Watch Learning Problems Disappear

The Power of Imagery

Watch Learning Problems Disappear

The Power of Imagery

by
Mildred Odess Gifford

The names of the people in this book have
been changed to protect their privacy.

Library of Congress Catalog Card Number 97-94692

ISBN 0-9661162-0-8

Manufactured in the United States of America
First printing 1998
Second printing 1999

Published by
Giffodess Books

In honor and memory of my daughter, Eleonore, who, upon reading some of these vignettes, said to me, "Ma, this is publishable."

This book is the result of her initial encouragement.

Acknowledgments

We stand upon the shoulders of others in gaining perspective and inspiration for our creations. Accordingly, I express my debt to the genius of two of my teachers: Dr. Win Wenger and Dr. Akhter Ahsen. I also learned much from Drs. Cecelia Pollack, Moshe Feldenkrais, Don Schuster, and Jean Houston.

I wish to acknowledge my husband, Charles Gifford, who assembled the book on his computer, and who put the art work together from various sources. Without his time and support, this book would not have been published.

In addition, I am indebted to my former colleague, Jack Berkman, for the many hours he spent editing. His careful proofreading and suggestions were invaluable.

As with the publication of many books, the suggestions and comments of friends and family are an essential part of the process, and to them all, I am grateful. These caring people are too numerous to mention, but I hope they will know that I remember and have not taken them for granted. Finally, I want to acknowledge my friend Vonnie, who, upon listening to accounts of my surprising experiences, first said to me, "Millie, you ought to write these down." And so I did.

Table of Contents

Detailed Table of Contents

Section One—Vignettes: Imagery

Chapter 1—Eidetic Imagery

Chapter 2—Visit Your Wise Being

Chapter 3—Mastering Skills and Concepts

Chapter 4—Language and Speaking Problems

Section Two—Vignettes: Student Attitudes and Behaviors

Chapter 5—The Experience of Being Learning Disabled

Chapter 6—"Hopeless" Students

Chapter 7—Disrespectful Behavior

Chapter 12—Discussing Values in the Classroom

Section Three: Communications

Chapter 13—Communication with Colleagues

Chapter 14—Feedback from Students

Post Scripts

Appendix

Some Procedures for Using Imagery in Learning

Bibliography

The Barricaded LD Student

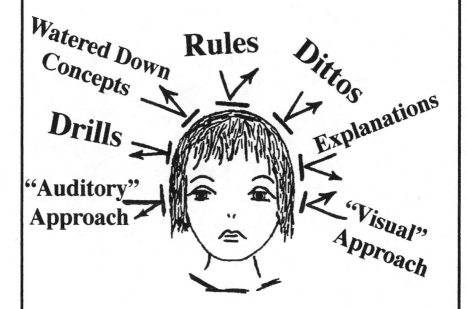

Watered Down Concepts

Rules

Dittos

Drills

Explanations

"Auditory" Approach

"Visual" Approach

M.G. '86

Preface

When I first became a teacher, other teachers would say to me, *"If they can't read above fourth-grade level by the time they're in high school, forget it."* Many ninth-graders came to me with levels well below fourth grade. I couldn't "forget it" and embarked upon an ongoing search for effective materials and methods. Meanwhile I taught them phonics. I also worked on their self-image by drawing upon my experiences in personal growth workshops. In these experiences, the participants and the leader would *interact* with each other, in contrast to conventional situations where the teacher speaks, and the students *react*.

I learned much along with my students. One thing I learned was that they often didn't recognize the humor I intended when I rolled my eyes in pretended (or actual) exasperation, or when I made a joke or a pun.

I also came to realize that students' negative behaviors often reflected upsetting incidents they had experienced at home or in prior classes. They may have refused a humiliating demand to read aloud and been punished for it. A well-intentioned teacher, insisting that **all** students take a turn at oral reading, may find herself unintentionally embroiled in a power struggle, not realizing that some students were refusing to submit to further insult from a system which had failed to educate them for nine or ten years.

I took a risk the first time I used visual imagery with students.

What if it didn't work? I was afraid of appearing foolish, but something that Jack Canfield had said at a workshop gave me the courage to try it. *If you're reluctant to try imagery with your class, remember, 'The only way to do it is to do it.'* That statement was all I needed in order to chance it.

Success thereafter was made possible through a combination of imagery and, what I have come to call, an *Aikido** attitude. In addition, I encountered an excellent phonics-based program called *Direct Instruction*, developed by Siegfried Engelmann and his associates. (Published by SRA)

After twenty-one years of experiments, failures, and successes, I had adapted and developed many methods and materials which I felt might be useful to other educators. As retirement approached, I felt like the breadwinner who had built a thriving business but had no children to take it over.

I decided, therefore, to record my experiences that I thought might be valuable to others. I have included vignettes which I found amusing, amazing, and/or touching. Some of these are presented more for their human interest or basic philosophical ideas than for their use as educational strategies. I hope other teachers will try the strategies and adapt those that appeal to them.

*Although most widely known as a martial art, the *Aikido* philosophy means that you accomplish your ends while blending harmoniously with the other person. For example, in combat if your opponent swings at you, you move away in the direction of his motion; thereby he falls from his own doing—not from your hitting back. Thus, there is no feeling of competition. In the teaching situation, if the teacher does not oppose the student, but instead respectfully allows him or her the choice of cooperating or not, the student will usually cooperate sooner or later. In any event, the teacher does not feel she has to "win", and a power struggle is avoided.

Introduction

Why Imagery?*

The sad fact that so many of our students fail to learn in spite of being in "special ed", should make us realize that the teachers themselves need to learn better methods and find more effective materials. This is not to discount the reality that the single most important factor for a student is a supportive home environment. However, while teachers are generally powerless to change a student's home environment, they are not necessarily powerless to make themselves into more successful teachers.

When we teach only through oral or written language, many students are unable to benefit, because they don't process language efficiently. Many of these students are unusually gifted in art, music, science, creative writing, etc. They typically respond well to instruction that utilizes imagery, music, rhythm, drama, and/or physical movement. Since these are methods which traditional teaching often ignores, some of our most gifted students are penalized.

The schools then call these students *learning disabled*. In addition to bearing the stigma of such labeling, these students suffer the terrible pain and frustration of failing to learn to read adequately. Einstein was a famous example of such a

Imagery: the act of forming images in the mind; visualization

student. He flunked out of his regular school, succeeding academically only after his parents put him into a school that used imagery. Later, he arrived at his famous discoveries through watching the "movies" in his mind. He'd watch the unfolding scenario of a problem about the behavior of light rays and would actually observe what would happen in his hypothetical situations.

I adopted this strategy when I needed to draw a picture of a boy holding his arm in a bent position. I couldn't get the arm to look right, so I visualized a real boy and noted the angle of the elbow and the proportions of the upper and lower arm. Then I opened my eyes and easily corrected the drawing.

In addition to becoming more effective teachers, we need to find alternatives to the drugs that entice many teen-agers. Adolescents can become healthier by learning wholesome ways to relieve tensions and alleviate anxieties, thereby strengthening their resistance to the allure of drugs. Imagery is one safe alternative.

A Few of the Areas Where Imagery Makes Learning Possible

[Detailed steps for some of the strategies are described in the vignettes. Others are found in the Appendix.]

- Installing Spelling Words in the Mind

- Recognizing Printed Words without Having to Spell Them First

- Remembering the Short Vowel Sounds

- Removing Blocks to Speech

- Understanding Verb Tenses

- Enabling Students to Understand and Remember What They Read.

- Relieving Anxiety before Tests or Other Stressful Situations.

- Increasing Awareness and Intelligence through *Image Streaming*.

- Solving Personal Problems

What Is Wholistic Education?

Many of the stories that follow illustrate a *wholistic* approach to education. What makes the wholistic, or *whole brain* approach different from more conventional teaching? Basically, it starts with the difference in how we regard the phenomenon of *learning*.

The Conventional Philosophy

Conventional educators often have an unquestioned faith in the IQ concept. They assume there are fixed limits to how much learning one individual can accumulate, so the mind is seen as a container which can "hold" only so much knowledge. Therefore, a student's potential is equated with an IQ number, and this equation influences the expectations and attitudes of teachers towards the students.

Even in cases where the teacher no longer subscribes to

this narrow attitude, conventional English and Reading lessons are still taught mainly through the use of language and logic. Thereby only a very limited area of the brain is addressed. Largely ignored are activities that would engage much more of the brain.

The Wholistic Philosophy

In the *wholistic* approach, the mind is regarded as virtually limitless, hampered mainly by negative suggestions or expectations. Importance is placed upon addressing as much of the two brain hemispheres as possible. In addition, the general health habits of the students may also be addressed, insofar as this latter factor influences the ability of students to learn. The student is regarded as a whole integrated being, rather than a collection of separate parts. Thus, stories, puppetry, roleplay, music, humor, physical movement, and of course imagery capture the students' attention, helping to develop both understanding and long-term memory. The students are not *trying* to understand the lesson and therefore are able to relax and absorb the information naturally, sometimes without even realizing it.

Subliminal factors are also taken into account. These include the physical and emotional environment, as well as the teacher's body language. Positive suggestion is important, along with the recognition that success breeds success.

In presenting the lessons, care is taken to integrate what might otherwise become splinters of unrelated, meaningless information. After first presenting an overview, the material is broken down into parts, experienced in a variety of ways, and then put back together as a meaningful whole. "Overview, Analysis, Synthesis" might be one way of describing the overall teaching structure.

Brief Explanation of Some Terms

We hear references to terms such as "imagery," "visualization," "suggestion," and "awareness"; but unless we have taken the time to read on these subjects or to attend workshops, these terms may have but a vague meaning for us. Therefore, I will very briefly discuss them.

Imagery: A general term that includes the act of seeing, hearing, and otherwise experiencing things in your mind.

Visualization: Seeing in your mind the idea, word, or diagram that is being taught. Some people have difficulty visualizing, but this skill can be developed through various strategies. (See the stories of Corman and Berna.) Reading comprehension problems disappear when the students are directed to close their eyes and visualize the scene of a story, sentence by sentence, if necessary.

Guided or Directed Imagery: Eyes closed, students see the scenes and the action unfold, under the teacher's directions. This process can be used to experience an episode in history, take an imaginary trip through the digestive tract, install spelling words in the mind, etc. The more senses that are used, the stronger will be the memory.

Creative Imagery: The stage is set by the teacher, but the discoveries come out of the student's own "unconscious" wisdom. Examples are the *Visit to Your Wise Being* (explained in a later chapter) and any variations the teacher may be inspired to devise.

Eidetic Imagery: Scenes are remembered or created through imaging so that the experience seems almost real. As the subject goes back several times over the same problem scene and re-experiences the process, the images progress as in a movie, and the problem spontaneously resolves itself.

Language Smoothing: (Win Wenger, *Making Your Language a Very, Very Fine Bed of Sand*, Psychegenics Press, 1985.) The student sees a familiar scene and describes it aloud in answer to the teacher's questions. Students who have trouble with oral language usually reply with one-word answers. The teacher then takes the one-word answer and expands it to a full sentence or two, followed by the student's echoing of the sentence(s) (with eyes still closed, viewing the scene.) I have used this strategy to break through severe language blocks. (See story of Arthur.)

Image Streaming: (Win Wenger, *How to Increase Your Intelligence*, Bobbs-Merrill, 1975; Dell Books, 1976.) For about ten minutes daily, the student describes a scene (preferably from Nature) to a partner or to a tape recorder. Wenger cites experiments with college students which resulted in an average increase of twenty points in IQ after two months.[See *Reinert, Charles P. in* bibliography at end of book.]

Suggestion: Too often we are blind to the value of suggestion and imagination. I have found that students can relax and learn more readily when I suggest that they see themselves with a white or golden light filling their minds. I tell them that the path between the hearing and seeing parts of their brain is now lit up, making it easy for them to understand what they hear and read.

Decoding: Reading a word by sounding out its letters.

The Vignettes

In many of these episodes I was working with a student one-on-one. Sometimes, if a student walked into class looking or sounding upset, I felt it would be unrealistic to expect her to concentrate on the lesson. In such a case, I sometimes would arrange for the class to work on lessons in a peer-tutoring mode (i.e. with a partner) or I would give them written work, while in a corner of the room, I attended to the needs of the student concerned.

In other cases, if I thought the activity or discussion would benefit everyone, I would include the whole class in the intervention. I believe that much valuable learning would have been missed, had I not sometimes interrupted my lesson plan and taken the time to work on the immediate need at hand.

In reading some of these vignettes, one might ask, *What does all this have to do with teaching English, reading, science, or with the development of academic skills?* I answer with the same rationale I would give my students: *Although this may be a reading class (or English, etc.) you will not learn well if you don't understand what people say, or if you can't express what you mean when you talk.* It is important to:

- know how to listen to others and to understand what they are saying;

- express yourself so that others will understand you;
- know how to think and to remember things;
- understand and respect yourself and others.

I therefore have included many episodes that aren't related directly to academic teaching, but which are indispensible to success in learning.

Feedback from Students

As part of their final exams, I frequently had my students write feedback messages,

In order to help them structure their feedback, I would usually write three or four questions on the board to get them started. Here are some examples of questions I would ask:

What did you learn this year in my class?

What did you like about this class?

What would you like to change about this class?

What was hard? What was easy? etc.

I have included feedback by students in some of the vignettes. Other feedbacks are given in Chapter Fourteen.

Section One

Vignettes: Imagery

Chapter One

Eidetic Imagery
A Brief Introduction

It was in a psychology course at college many years ago that I first heard of *eidetic imagery*. At that time I understood it to be the equivalent of photographic memory, but have since learned that that is only one form. The other form of eidetics is the *structural* form and is noted for its ability to effect remarkable therapeutic change. When I adapted its use to my teaching, I was amazed at the results and it became an essential part of my teaching, enabling students to succeed in situations normally regarded as hopeless.

Akhter Ahsen, the founder and acknowledged leader of Eidetic Imagery Therapy, states in "Eidetics: An Overview" (*Journal of Mental Imagery*, Spring, 1977, Vol. 1) that *in the image is the cure*. Through visualizing scenes or objects, one experiences new and important understandings of a subject or a past event. This activity is surprisingly effective in helping students discover more appropriate ways to behave or to learn material that they had, until now, failed to understand.

The eidetic can be described as a visual image which is seen in the mind with profound vividness. It is accompanied by feelings, as well as a sense of meaning. Whereas there are some who might fear that "seeing things in your mind" is a sign of madness, or at least is dangerous, Ahsen states that the total experience in all its dimensions is in no way pathological. When sane persons use imagery, they know that the image is in their minds and is not real. Alport similarly emphasized the "healthful" structure of the eidetic (*ibid.*).

Ahsen writes in *Learning Ability and Disability: An Image Approach* (Brandon House, Inc., 1992) *"It is our belief that imagery, which has been by and large overlooked, offers a remarkable scientific and social synthesis of the new direction in education, which is demanding that the field reevaluate itself and stretch itself into the future with new understanding of the tools in their hands."* Ahsen says eidetic imagery is the hub to which all other imageries relate.

In my classroom, I have repeatedly experienced the truth of the following statement by Ahsen: *"Although a person thinks he does not know something, it quietly awaits recognition through experiencing the drama of the eidetic imagery process. When the images are enacted and the process of learning is initiated, discovery takes place constantly." (ibid)*

The following examples illustrate some of the uses of eidetic imagery as a learning and personal growth tool:

Evan
Five-Minute Eidetic Therapy

Evan remarked that his back was sore, because yesterday he had started lifting weights again. I invited him to try some imagery, as follows:

"Picture yourself getting ready to lift the weights. Watch very

closely what you do first. Notice the position of your feet, your hips, your hands, your shoulders, your head, etc. [Pause between each part.]

"What part of your body moves first?

"In slow motion, run the movie of lifting the weights. Feel what your legs are doing, your arms, pelvis, chest, back, neck, head. Take your time. If something feels strained, stop. Figure out how to move so that it will be both smooth and easy.

"Do this many times over, until it's perfect."

Within about five minutes he opened his eyes. He said the pain was completely gone. I was surprised. I thought it would take longer.

Tom's Prank

Tom, following the latest fashion in pranks, had pulled down Nardo's sweat pants in their math class. Nardo told me about it the next day, saying that he had been terribly embarrassed.

Later, during my planning time, I asked Tom's math teacher to send him to my room. When I asked Tom about the episode, he repeated Nardo's story with amusement and with no recognition of the latter's embarrassment. I felt that if I lectured him about Nardo's humiliation, he might not really "get it." I suggested, therefore, that he do an imagery exercise, hoping it would help him recognize Nardo's feelings. He consented. I directed him to visualize a stage play of the incident and simultaneously report aloud to me what he was viewing. In other words, he was to be both the actor and the narrator in the play.

Tom's Imagery

I asked him to close his eyes and see himself in math class. I then instructed him to describe the episode to me as it was happening. He related the scene rapidly, and when I asked how each of them was feeling, he said that he and Nardo were laughing.

I had him repeat the imaging two more times, in slow motion. At the end of each scene, I told him to take a break, and (mentally) go out into the fresh air and sunshine and breathe in the healthful, invigorating air. Then we resumed the play. Each time, Tom reported more details, as described in the following scenes:

Second Imaging

During this second viewing, Tom reported that Nardo's face was red. I asked how Nardo was feeling this time, and he replied, "He's laughing." He said that he, Tom, was also laughing, meaning that he was amused.

Third Imaging

On the next viewing he said that Nardo's face was red, and he was shaking his head. He replied to my questions by saying that Nardo was embarrassed, and that he himself was feeling "shameful."

I was elated that the experience had enabled Tom to understand how his prank had made Nardo feel. I'm sure that learning from his own mind was far more effective than any amount of discussion could have been.

When the exercise was finished, I asked Tom if he planned

to do anything about what had happened, and he answered that he intended to apologize to Nardo.

This episode is one example of several imagery experiences for Tom. When he was a freshman, he was abnormally naive socially, but by the time he became a senior, he had matured into a thoughtful and respectful young man.

Monte Learns to Trust His Feelings

Sometimes an interaction can result in unexpected learning for the teacher as well as for the student. In the following episode, the student learned that he could acknowledge his feelings and still be safe. Consequently, his behavior became more open and relaxed during lessons.

The teacher, on the other hand, learned (from the student's imagery) about the risks that teen-agers may face. She learned that, even though one is innocent, running away from police can sometimes be the wiser action.

Quiet and polite, Monte is a tall, good-looking ninth-grader. He is quite proud, and if a teacher wrongly accuses him of a misdeed, he will deny it—once. If the teacher doubts his word, he remains silent, refusing to convince her of his innocence.

Another of his characteristics is his refusal to talk or write about his feelings or personal affairs. I noticed, however, that in reading class when we brainstormed words for some point of language, he would offer words like "kill," "punch," "shoot," etc.

One day he happened to mention that the police had mistaken him for a person who was dealing drugs. Both he and the drug-dealing youth were wearing similar clothes. The police called to him, and he ran and got away. I asked what he thought would have happened had he not run away, and he indicated that they would have mistreated him, even though he had done nothing wrong.

Thinking that he was mistaken, I asked if he'd be willing to do some imagery to help discover further understanding. When he emphatically refused, I asked if he was afraid that seeing pictures in his head would make him crazy. He agreed that that was what he feared.

I then explained that when people are afraid to acknowledge frightening or painful thoughts, they sometimes repress them. They push the thoughts down into the unconscious mind, just as you might lock a frightened animal in the cellar. However, the more they are locked in, or repressed, the more violent the thoughts become, and the harder they try to break out. Finally, they can get so wild and desperate that they break down the repressing door—and burst into awareness in the form of extremely scary pictures and words, which a person might be unable to distinguish from reality.

On the other hand, facing the thoughts and fears may be the safer thing to do. When you allow a trained person to *help* you see the pictures, you are safeguarding yourself. And that's the difference between *crazy* pictures and healthy ones. He consented to try it.

I proceeded to have him mentally experience the scene with the police, but this time he was to imagine himself stopping when they called to him. Here is the account of his imaged experience:

After I stopped for the police, they got out of their cars and slammed me up against a pole. They searched me and found nothing. Then they put me into the police car and took me to the police station, where they questioned me about the other kid. I refused to talk, so they locked me in a cell.

Monte explained to me that he refused to talk because they would have hounded him for information from then on. He indicated that he felt claustrophobic and frightened in the jail cell.

When Monte was finally released and went home, he reported that his mother was yelling at him. I asked, *"How do you feel as she's yelling at you?"*

"Good!" was his enthusiastic response.

He sat with eyes closed, not talking, for a long time. Finally, I indicated it was time to end the exercise. He opened his eyes, looked at his watch, and shook his head in disbelief. *"I thought it was two or three hours!"* he said. In reality, the whole exercise had taken about ten minutes.

Then he remarked that he had a headache. Back to imagery. I asked him to look at the headache and to describe its characteristics: location, shape, size, color, volume (*how much water could you pour into it?*), temperature, etc. I repeated this series of questions, and after the second time around, he said the headache was gone. *"What did you do?"* he asked. I pointed out that by paying attention to the pain instead of trying to avoid it, he was able to relax and let go of it.

A few days later, for the first time, he mentioned his father to me. He volunteered that if his father were alive, Monte would be put into a strict school where they'd make him work. He said his father had died when Monte was five years old, and he acknowledged that he felt very bad about that. He really missed him. His father was a boxer and had wanted him to be one also.

I asked if that was what he, Monte, wanted, and he said

"*no*." I pointed out that fathers often think their little boys are copies of themselves, especially when they're only five years old. If Father could see him now, he'd realize that Monte was different, and he wouldn't want him to be a boxer if he didn't like that. This comment seemed to satisfy him.

A week or so later, I remarked to Monte that he seemed more relaxed and asked if that was true. He said that he did feel that way. Perhaps it was the imaging that had allowed him to trust me enough to share his deep feelings. The resultant trust had created in him a more relaxed attitude in my class.

Overcome Difficulty Seeing Printed Words
Focusing the Internal Vision

I have found that many learning disabled students are unstable in directionality habits, and sometimes they will look at a word backwards, that is, from right to left. Thus, you will hear errors such as the oft-mentioned *was* for *saw*, etc.

However, a more frustrating and mystifying experience is to witness a student reciting a word which has absolutely no relationship to the *printed* word that he is looking at; i.e., there are no letters in common between the written and the spoken word, nor is the spoken word a synonym for the written. The student behaves as though she really doesn't see the word in question, and recites, instead, a word that is elsewhere (or nowhere) on the page. I assume that many a teacher has scolded in exasperation, *"LOOK at the word! Can't you SEE it?"*

How does one account for such strange behavior? It really does seem as though the student is blind. The reality is, however, that although the student is *not* blind, she is not focusing her eyes correctly for reading! She will, however, be able to read the word successfully if I tell her to visualize the letters first and then read the word from the mental image.

Obviously one can't continually interrupt reading to transfer every problematic word into a mental image. I devised some strategies which resulted in more accurate seeing and reading. The following are examples of this strategy, which I call *brief mental movies:*

Strategies for Focusing the Eyes; One Example

When Barbie first entered my ninth-grade class, she was reading at a first- grade level. Even after I taught her phonics rules, she still displayed extreme difficulty with reading. She would misread a word that she could easily recognize or figure out, were she perceiving it accurately. If I spelled the word aloud while she closed her eyes and mentally wrote the letters, she would correctly read the word from the mental image. Without the imaging strategy, however, she was unable to correct her errors, even after repeated attempts.

One day during the lesson, I remembered a talk by Dr. Ahsen. He had mentioned that when learning disabled students visualize their parents standing in front of them, the parents are usually seen far apart from each other, whereas most other people will see the parents standing close together.

Ahsen indicates that the wide distance between the imaged parents makes it impossible for the viewer to focus on them both at the same time. Thus, they are seen internally with the *peripheral* vision.

This mode of seeing extends to the way these individuals view the external world as well. Obviously, such a style of seeing will interfere with the ability to focus dependably upon written material. Therefore, we observe some learning disabled students reading as though they don't see some of the letters, losing their place, and appearing frustratingly unsure.

Since nothing else was working with Barbie, I decided to try, in a direct manner, to change Barbie's mental focus from a peripheral to a central one.

I halted the lesson and asked the students to close their eyes and to see their parents standing in front of them. The other students in the class, who could read with much less frustration than Barbie, saw their parents relatively close together. Barbie, however, saw her mother about two feet in front of her, while her father was far *behind* her!

I planned to have her alter the image so the father would stand next to the mother but thought it might be easier if I did it in two stages. When I asked Barbie to have her father stand next to herself first, she replied, "I don't *want* my father near me!" (Her father is very strict; she is afraid of him.)

I assured her that it was only an image and not real life. She then complied and nodded her head when it was done. After I had the father move next to the mother, I told her to take a good look at the picture. Then I told her to open her eyes and read. To my delight she read the passage without a single mistake! I advised her to view the image as many times as possible every day for the next several days. I worried that it would prove to be just a one-time fluke.

The next day her new-found success continued. Each time that she read, I instructed her to keep the image in her mind. The following week I heard her reading orally to herself—

perfectly. When she became aware that I was listening, she made a couple of mistakes. *Keep Mother and Father in front*, I said. Then she continued to read, this time very well. I reminded her to continue seeing the image a hundred times a day.

During my planning periods, I worked with her a few times to reinforce the new learning. I expanded the imagery experiences to include scenes with her brother, who was to enter the room and offer to do her homework for her. When Ahsen described this image, he said that the sibling always enters from the right, and that the student is to image herself pushing the brother (or sister) away, by gesturing toward the right.. Without this gesture, she will passively try to escape his interference by moving her eyes away from him; i.e., to the left, thus accounting for the tendency of many dyslexic students to look at words from right to left.

I wondered, "How does Ahsen know the sibling will always approach from the right? What if there is no sibling?" Ahsen's response is to substitute someone instead of the sibling.

I asked Barbie to point in the direction from which her brother had entered. Contrary to my expectations, she indicated her left instead of her right! I stuck with the exercise, however, by telling her to see him approach and stand by the side of her desk. When I asked her where he was standing, she pointed to her *right*! I was much relieved.

I then instructed her to say, "Go away," gesturing with her right hand. She was to repeat this scene many times. (I recently used this imagery with a dyslexic adult, and to my dismay, the interfering brother stood to the *left* of her desk instead of to the right. I told her to watch him walk in front of her desk toward her right. Then I had her gesture with her hand to push him further away toward the right. After this, the woman picked up the book to read and reported that her eyes felt noticeably more comfortable than before.)

I devised other imaging strategies for Barbie, one example being the *Target Practice* which I describe in the vignette about Millicent.

The lessons continued to go well. When I re-tested her a few months later, she scored at a high fourth-grade level.

I was concerned that she might regress over the summer, but in the fall, Barbie showed that she had retained the growth. The planning team moved her into mainstream social studies and English for the second semester. Although she retained the reading gains she had made, Barbie encountered serious family troubles and consequently was absent from school a great portion of the year. As a result, she missed the opportunity to further improve her reading skill, as well as to pass her other courses and be promoted to the twelfth grade.

Circumstances were no better the following year. I had retired by then and learned that she was getting early dismissal from school because she had a job. The next thing I heard was that she had quit school. I felt very sad about that and could only wonder if the job had prevented her from experiencing academic success, thus encouraging her to give up altogether. It's a poor idea for a learning disabled student to hold a job outside of school.

Feedback from Barbie—Grade Ten

The thing that was most helpful for me was the imagery. Some kids didn't think that was helpful for them but it was for me.

I learn how to read better and decode word.
To be tureful [truthful] I did find nothing boring.
The thing that I find hard was the syllbale.
I enjoy most of all the thing that you told me to do.
I like the way you teach.
I would[n't] like you to change anything.
Thank [you] for being a good teacher to me.

P.S. I later learned from a colleague that Barbie had entered the Community College. She is bright and should do well.

Focusing the Eyes—Alternative Strategy

As an alternative to the *Parental Images* exercise, I devised another scenario called *Target Practice*. This avoids the emotional component which may cause some students to resist the parental imaging.

Target Practice

Millicent was having severe difficulty reading aloud. She would read the first sentence correctly, but on the next one, her words would have no relation to what was written. She would continue that way, alternating between accuracy and total unrelatedness. After a few minutes, I stopped the oral reading to try an exercise that had just occurred to me. I call it *Target Practice Imagery*.

First, we discussed targets, and how they are used in archery. Then, on the chalkboard, I had Millicent draw a target with a bull's eye, indicating the point which the arrow was supposed to hit.

After she sat down, I had the entire class close their eyes

and participate mentally in the following scene:

See yourself standing on a large lawn of green grass. You are looking at a target, a little distance away. You are holding a bow and arrow.

Nod your head when you see the scene.

Now shoot the arrow at the target. Observe where it hits. Raise your hand after you shoot, and get ready to tell me where on the target it landed. Do not fool me; tell the truth.

Millicent went to the board and indicated a spot three circles away from the bull's eye. None of the other students hit the bull's eye either.

Next I instructed them to return to the mental scene.

See a waterfall of cool, fresh, sparkling water nearby. Take a refreshing drink. Nod your head when you finish.

Now pick up your bow and arrow. Look at the bull's eye. Now look at the point of the arrow, and back at the bull's eye. Do this two more times.

*In your mind, see a line from the tip of the arrow **straight** to the bull's eye.*

Now shoot the arrow, and raise your hand when finished.

Where did it land?

In every case, the students reported hitting the center of the target. Before we returned to the oral reading, I asked Millicent to repeat the mental target practice. She said her eyes hurt, so I dropped the request.

When the oral reading resumed, Millicent read her paragraph perfectly, except for leaving off a final *s* and *ed*. I was thrilled, as was she. I advised her to image the activity once each day and again before bedtime, not daring to tell her to do it more often, for fear of eye strain. Later, I checked with a developmental optometrist, who complimented my work and assured me she could not harm her eyes by doing the exercise.

In the next class, Corman was finding it impossible to keep his place during the oral reading. Each time that it was his turn to read, he'd start in the wrong place. I stopped the lesson and had the class do the *Target Practice*. When we resumed, to my delight Corman excelled at keeping his place, missing not even once. In fact, his reading was the best in the class.

Explanatory Theory

Many learning disabled students exhibit difficulty keeping their place while reading. Even when they do keep their place, it is common for them to leave out the end or the beginning sounds of words. It's as though they don't see these letters. Sometimes, while reading a sentence, they will say a word that is above or below the target word, or is elsewhere on the page.

The teacher may be prone to ask. *"Why don't you pay attention? Why don't you point to each word to help you keep your place?"* **Perhaps the students refuse to point because focusing is so difficult.**

I remind the students to do the target imagery whenever I think they are going to have trouble keeping their place or focusing. Millicent has been conscientiously doing her imagery practice at home and continues to have success.

Corman, however, still needs reminding and doesn't do the imaging at home. He no doubt would benefit from private sessions in which I would have him see himself doing the exercise many times every day. The idea of this "rehearsing" would be to enhance the chance of his following through with the imaging on a daily basis. (More on Corman in other Sections.)

Roger

Roger was born when his mother was fifteen years old and his father was sixteen or seventeen. He told me that his grandmother considered her daughter too young to care for him, so he was shifted around from one relative to another all his life. He was told that his father never once came to see him, even when Roger was an infant.

At fifteen, he entered my ninth-grade class, reading at the second-grade level. I was delighted when I first met him. He was attractive and appeared more intelligent than most of the students. I could speak to him in normal language, instead of using a watered-down vocabulary. It soon became evident, however, that he was frequently upset and depressed, and at these times, he would ignore the lesson or ask to see the adjustment specialist. Consequently, he missed many of my classes.

I spent many of my preparation periods trying to help him cope with the stresses of his life, and he seemed to appreciate it. However, I felt hopeless about his reading, since he attended class so rarely. After his uncle asked him to leave, he went to live with a cousin, and he began missing school.

When he showed up for a make-up exam, I had him do

imagery instead of the exam. After a short time, Roger spontaneously picked up his book and began reading the exam lesson aloud with no trouble at all. He read the six subsequent passages. Although I skipped the accompanying instructions and drill, he read every story without a single mistake, something that had never happened before. *It was obvious that he did not need much further instruction. His main need was to learn to focus his eyes reliably on the material.*

Roger Threatens to Walk Out of Class

Roger retained his reading gains over the summer. During his second year in high school, his behavior was a little more mature; i.e., he no longer disrupted the lesson when he felt out-of-sorts. However, he still got upset easily. At such times, he either sat quietly without participating in the lesson, or else he asked permission to see the adjustment specialist. The first time that I refused permission, he threatened to walk out anyway. I held my ground, relying upon our good relationship to keep him from defying me. He remained in the room, although he spent the period quietly drawing. It was apparent that he was listening to the lesson, because when the other students didn't understand a point, he would volunteer the answer without looking up.

Roger's Stomach Pain

Roger had a history of coming to class and complaining of aches and pains on an almost daily basis. Early on, I realized that he handled emotional distress by translating it into physical pain. One day he entered class, sat down, and writhing in his seat with a look of agony on his face, began moaning that his stomach was "killing him."

While the student teacher conducted the lesson, I spoke quietly to Roger. I said that the light from the sun is God's magical tool, and we can use this tool to heal our pain. It is not necessary to "believe in God" to have this work.

Just allow the golden rays of the sun to shine on your stomach. Let the rays go through and around your stomach. (I repeated this suggestion several times in similar ways.)

As I was speaking, Roger's facial expression relaxed. He opened his eyes and began participating in the lesson, mentioning not another word of complaint.

My theory: Allowing the light to shine on and through his stomach had the effect of relaxing his muscles, thereby relieving the tension and pain.

Roger's Feedback

The imagery were the most helpful thing.
I learn how to use imagery to help me Read and thing [think].
The consonants were boring.
Some of the vowel sounds were hard.
I enjoy the vowel sounds also because they were a great experience. I don't tink it cold [could] *be better because it is a good class all ready.*

Chapter Two

Visit Your "Wise Being"

Imagery can help individuals discover knowledge and wisdom which they didn't know they had. Students can use this strategy to solve personal problems and to learn more mature ways of behaving. Here are some illustrative episodes.

Monte Decides against Violence

Monte appeared quiet and depressed and was not participating in the lesson. Since my student teacher was present, I was able to take Monte into the corridor to hear what was wrong. Visibly upset, he told me the following story:

*A man who lived in "The Projects" had stolen some items from the apartment of Monte's cousin. Monte believed that the man was trying to break into **his** family's apartment also, because the lock had been tampered with.*

When Monte and his older brother confronted the man, he at first denied any guilt, and then said that the stuff was sold already. Monte's brother beat him up, and later the man said he was going to go to the apartment of Monte's girlfriend and "spit in her face." Monte said he would kill him if that happened.

Since it was clear that he wasn't speaking metaphorically, I suggested that Monte consult his inner *Wise Being*. We went to the library and sat in a private section. I introduced Monte to the procedure in the following manner:

"We have different parts to our minds. There's the part that acts like a little child and likes to be silly; there's the angry part that often gets us into trouble; and there's the wise part that knows a lot and can solve problems. Through imagery, I will help you talk with this wise part, which we will call your Wise Being.

The first step is for you to form a question about your problem. You will ask it of the Wise Being later."

Monte thought of a question but chose not to reveal it to me. Now we were ready to begin our adventure. I spoke to him as follows:

"See yourself in a beautiful place. . . Relax and look around. . . Breathe in the fresh air. . . Feel it soft on your skin. . . See the colors around you. . . Listen to any sounds. . . Smell the freshness of the air. . . Notice where you are standing. . . Look up and see a mountain far in the distance, with a castle on it. . . Now see a cloud floating towards you in the blue sky. . . It settles down around you like a soft white blanket and then floats up again, carrying you in it. Up, up it floats, higher and higher, and begins to drift toward the mountain."

I ask questions, such as *"Do you feel it?"* or *"Do you see it?"* to check that he's following along. In response he raises a hand or a finger to show he is ready to continue.

"The cloud reaches the mountain. . . It settles on the ground in front of your own private castle. You get out and walk to the door. Feel the door. Notice what it's made of. . . How does it smell? . . . Now put your hand on the handle, open it

and step inside. . . See your Wise Being. . . Where is the Wise One, near the door or at the other end of the room?"

Monte's answer indicates that he is keeping up with the things I'm saying. I don't use gender pronouns, because I want to avoid influencing or interfering with the image.

"Now you and your Wise Being see each other. . . You hug and feel much love. . . Now you ask your question. . . Let me know when you have done so. . . Then, in answer to your question, the Wise Being reaches behind a screen and hands you something. . .Do you see what it is?". . . Monte nods his head. *"Thank your Wise Being. . . You hug each other again. . . Your Wise Being says, 'Remember that I'm always here, waiting for you. Please come back often.' . . . You go out of the castle and see the cloud waiting for you. . . It carries you back to the ground where you started from. . . Now you examine the gift. . . Do you see it? . . . What is it?"*

"A bottle."

"What's in the bottle?" I asked.

"A white paper."

"Anything on the paper?"

"No, just a blank white paper."

"What does it mean?"

"It means if I do what I was planning to do, my future will be a blank, just like the paper."

Monte opened his eyes and shook his head several times. Then we returned to the class, and he joined the others, cheerful and light-hearted, a total change from his previous worried state.

Sara Stops Feeling Alienated

Sara was a ninth-grader who appeared emotionless and uninvolved with the other students, except to make defensive and complaining remarks. She was very stout and seemed unhappy.

One day I suggested that she try a visit to her Wise Being. First I had her breathe deeply and relax her neck, stomach, heart, etc. Then I told her to see herself in a beautiful place. She was to feel the sunlight on her skin, smell the wonderful fresh air, hear any sounds, etc.

I next pointed out a fluffy cloud that was floating toward her. It landed at her feet, surrounded her, and proceeded to carry her gently to her castle on a distant mountain. There she received a gift from her Wise Being.

> *"It don't make no sense, but it was a heart,"* was her report after the imagery was over. She came out of it smiling, rubbing her eyes. I asked her to describe the gift.
> *"Just a heart."*
> "A real heart? Flesh and blood?" I asked.
> *"Yes."*

When she could find no meaning in the gift, I offered the following interpretation: *"The heart is Love. Your real heart is full of love, but it has been frozen tight. You don't want to feel the pain, so you closed up your heart."* There were tears in her eyes throughout the interpretation.

"When you close up your heart, you close your brain, too. You can allow your heart to relax and love, because you are

lovable. Even if others are mean and blind, you know your Wise Being loves you." I continued, *"When life gets too much for you, see the heart and your Wise Being who loves you. This can remind you that you are good and lovable and precious."*

I then advised her to visit her Wise Being every day, before school and at bedtime, and to appreciate her gift of the beautiful heart and its message.

At the conclusion of the experience, she looked relaxed and proceeded to participate in the classwork, behaving in a comfortable, friendly manner toward the other students. I felt gratified.

Note: *In principal, I believe one should not interpret someone else's dreams or images. However, when the imager is baffled and desires an interpretation, it is permissible to offer an obvious symbolism. The imager, of course, must stay aware of whether the interpretation fits his feelings, and reject any outside explanation that feels false.*

Dealing with the Blues— Walley Sees His Answer

Walley was a cooperative and motivated student, but on this particular day he was completely distracted. When I spoke to him, he appeared not to notice. When pressed, he gave me a blank look and mumbled, *"Yes, Ms. Gifford."*

In response to my questions, he said that he'd had enough sleep last night, but that something was bothering him. He indicated that he'd like to find out what it was, so I offered to help him visit his Wise Being.

After the imagery experience was over, Walley returned from his "visit," smiling happily.

"That was very good. Thank you, Ms. Gifford."
"Did you find out what was bothering you?"
"Yes."
"Would you like to tell us about it?"
"Well, there's this girl I like. And I was talking to her this morning—but then I got nervous and ran away. And I was sorry. That's what was bothering me."
"Did your Wise Being tell you that?"
*"The girl **was** my Wise Being. She gave me a paper that said a lot of nice things on it. And I'm going to see her and explain why I ran away. I feel much better. Thank you, Ms. Gifford."*

Marie Deals with Her Frightening Experience

Marie came to me before class to tell me about a frightening experience. Over the week-end an unknown man rang their doorbell, and her father did not answer it. Later, her mother saw a man jump onto their back porch, and then he disappeared. This happened again the next day.

Marie was worried that something bad might happen to her mother or father. Since they don't know who the man is, she feels there is no point in going to the police; the neighbors won't help, even if they know who the man is. She says he knows the times they go to church, come home, etc.

I suggested she visit her Wise Being to see if she could get some good advice. She agreed, and this is the message that she received:

The Wise Being told her to speak to the police on the beat and tell them what times the man came around. She hadn't thought of this before, nor had I.

Note: After this, I heard no more about the incident.

Drop Out or Stay in School?

Besides being "learning disabled," Paul displayed more than the usual amount of distracted and nervous behavior. Most of the time he paid no attention to the lesson, preferring to show off for the other students. He had severe acne on his face, and in this area, at least, I could make a small start toward helping him. After I referred him to the school social worker, arrangements were made for treatment by a doctor. His skin cleared up completely, and perhaps that was the one real impetus he needed in order to begin to change his behavior.

Because Paul had difficulty focusing on the academic lessons, much time was spent on personal growth experiences. However, his handwriting and concentration skills remained impossible, as well as his ability to behave calmly in a dependable way. On more than one occasion, I reminded him that vile language and a hot temper were not only unacceptable, but were not really macho.

The following fall, however, I was delighted to find him a much calmer and better-behaved young man. He'd met a girl in a distant city, and they were talking about getting married after he graduated. Although he still had fits of depression and moodiness, he displayed much more concentration and courtesy and even began getting good grades in his other classes. (An *A* in a mainstream class in American History!) An extended trip to visit his girlfriend in the middle of the school year, however, resulted in his failing one of the classes which he needed in order to graduate.

Two additional events contributed further to his slipping academic performance: he got a job that occupied his full time after school, and he bought a car. Many were the annoyed lectures he heard from me about the foolishness of childish persons having cars!

The Story of Paul's Imagery Gifts

It was the last week of classes in June. Paul was discouraged over the fact that if he wanted to have a high school diploma, he'd have to return to school for another year. We'd all had it with school by then, and I was no more inclined to teach a lesson than the students were able to listen.

When Paul shared his problem, therefore, I announced that we were all going to help him. The class agreed to do some imagery to get helpful (metaphoric) gifts for Paul. I then guided the class to visit their Wise Beings, and each student (in imagination) asked for a gift. Afterwards, Paul was the first to share his experience:

"I saw a letter, folded up. I opened it and on it, it said, 'Trust yourself. Don't be scared. Give it everything you've got. You will be successful.'"

One student saw *"a round ring—very shiny red stone in the middle—very shiny."*

Patricia saw *"money."* *"How much?"* I asked.
"I don't know. It was round and silver."

Jim saw *"a blue paper. Flowers all around. Words on the paper said, 'Try your best.'"*

When Paul did not find symbolic meanings in the gifts, I offered him the following impressions:

- Red *(stone in the ring) stands for courage. So whenever you start to feel scared, think of the ring, and it will give you courage.*

- *The* Silver Coin *will help you to feel rich enough so that you don't have to take a job after school and not have time for homework.* (A grin of recognition crossed his face at this comment.)

- Blue *stands for loyalty, so use it to help you trust yourself.*

- *You will be successful, because you will try your best, as Jim's blue paper says.*

- *The flowers around the edge of the paper will help you to be happy.*

Paul looked gratified, and I suggested that he make a poster illustrating the gifts. He agreed to do that.

P.S. *Paul did return in the fall and graduated the following June.*

Feedback: Essay Part of Paul's Final Exam

1. *I did not even know what was a head of me when i arive at Hartford High school I came across an intelegent teacher who teach me what i dint even know such ass pronuoncing letters and not Being scare of linhing* [learning?] *and Seaying* [seeing] *a cristol Bright light* [in imagination, for helping to

focus attention], *and the story about the captain C, and not Being afraid of stiking* [sticking] *out my toung and pronuncing letters* [th] *and I learn to put every capitol letter in front of every sentence.*

2. *the thing i like about this class is that the kids in this class are helpfull and they are a good group to work with and the teacher understand what the person means and sometime is a good quiet room to work in i like this classroom Because is good caring people.*

3. *I would like to Be forced to work soo i would not Be layzy and i don't like to full around when i'm trying to do my work and i wish i could learn more in this class room so when i go out in to the wold on my own i could do what i want.*

Jim's Message from His Wise Being

Jim, a student from Guyana, asked me if I thought he should drop out of school and go into the army to finish his education. I suggested that he ask his own Wise Being what to do. Here is a report of his experience, as told to me afterward in his own words:

I got a blue ribbon from my smart person. And I thank him for it.

Then I went back down [from the mountain].

Then I place the box on the floor.

Then, Mrs. Gifford ask me to place my forehead on the box and try to get a feeling what is in the box.

And then I get a feeling it was a document.
Mrs. Gifford ask me to read the document. I couldn't.

Then she ask me to put my forehead on the document and don't try to read it, but get a feeling what did it say.

And then the document said it's not a smart idea to do, and you don't ready for the army yet.

At the bottom of the document it said, To Jim.

Note: Jim's reading went from a pre-primer level to a fourth-grade level in one school year!

Chapter Three

Mastering Skills and Concepts

Introducing Imagery to Students

Before using imagery for the first time, students usually respond well to the following type of explanation:

"One goal of this course is to strengthen the language parts of your brain. These parts include listening, speaking, reading, spelling, writing, and thinking. To succeed in strengthening these parts, you will have to exercise your brain, and using imagery is probably the most effective and easiest way.

"However, you may feel worried that seeing pictures in your mind could be dangerous. Perhaps you know someone who is mentally ill, and he or she sees or hears things that aren't really there. They have no control over their imagination. The difference between ill persons and healthy ones is that the healthy persons know the difference between an imagined picture and a real one and, furthermore, they use their minds to become healthier and smarter.

"How does imaging help you to become smarter? For one thing, you rehearse in your mind the thing you're trying to

learn. For example, if you're learning to spell a word, you will be more successful if you write it mentally three times. That is how you put it into your memory bank. Then when you need to write the word, you look in your memory bank and see it. Good spellers automatically see the words in their mind. If you're not a good speller, that is how you can train yourself.

"A good way to develop a strong mind is to get into the habit of imaging every day. In addition, you will be surprised to find that by doing this when you have a problem, you can find your own answers. The only way that some of you can believe this is by actually trying it, so why not take a chance?"

Jules Discovers the Purpose of Reading

Many students have difficulty learning the sounds of letters (phonics) or understanding what they're reading (comprehension) but, surprisingly, there are some people who don't even realize that the printed words **have** any meaning.

Jules was one of these people. He was a ninth-grader who could barely read on a first-grade level in spite of my carefully structured lessons. He was quite naive socially, and the students didn't seem to take him seriously.

One day, Jules was trying to read aloud from a simple one-page story and having a terrible time of it. I stopped him after the first sentence and asked him to see in his mind a picture of what he had just read. He did so and then opened his eyes and re-read the sentence. A look of great surprise appeared on his face. It was clear that, until now, he hadn't realized that reading was connected to anything meaningful. Then, to *everyone's* surprise, he read the whole page with no difficulty. From then on, he made rapid progress. I wasted no time informing his other teachers that he could learn, and that they should take him seriously.

Note: Jules is an example of many students who become lost because of our failure to recognize that they misunderstand some very basic concept that most of us take for granted.

Berna

Berna's records from the middle school bilingual program indicated that she read on a sixth-grade level, a relatively high level for an inner-city learning disabled student. I was surprised, therefore, that she was scheduled into my lowest (English) reading class.

I soon realized, however, that Berna was in no way misplaced. In fact, I discovered that she actually read at only the second-grade level and didn't even know the names and sounds of many of the letters of the alphabet.

Sometimes when I asked her a question, she would simply look at me as though I had said nothing. She would just sit and look up as though waiting for I-know-not-what. Then I'd say, *"Why don't you answer me?"* to which she would respond by asking *"What?"* as though she'd been totally unaware that I had spoken earlier.

In the current episode, I was drilling her and another student on some words that ended with *ts*. Berna couldn't get the word *hats* and kept saying *hast* in spite of all my attempts to "open her eyes".

Finally, I decided to install the word in her visual imagery and have her read it directly from her mind. I said I was going to spell some letters, and she was to close her eyes and

imagine herself writing them on the chalkboard. She immediately said she couldn't do it.

"What stops you?" I asked.

"Thoughts," she responded. So I told her that that was all
right. She could just pretend she was writing the letters as I
named them. That satisfied her, and she then closed her eyes
and listened as I spelled "h-a-t-s."

I proceeded to recite the letters several more times, instruct-
ing her to write them each time again, on top of the same
letters that she wrote the first time. Eventually, she would
see the letters get sharp and clear. As I spelled, I watched her
finger tracing each letter on the table, while her eyes remained
closed.

When she finally indicated that she could see the letters
that she had written, I asked her to spell the word back to me.
When I asked her what the word said, she correctly read (eyes
still closed) *"hats."*

I then had her write the letters *B-e-r-n-a*. She was able to
see the image after three dictations, and easily announced,
"Berna".

Next came an unusual happening: I dictated the letters *"D-
i-a-z."* She couldn't recognize her own last name, even after
six dictations and correctly spelling it back to me. I had her
open her eyes and look at her signature on her paper. *"Diaz,"*
she said. Then her eyes widened with surprise. She closed
her eyes again to see the word in her mind and then opened
them and looked at it on the paper. The concept dawned upon
her: *what she saw in her mind was related to what she saw
on the paper!*

She was enthusiastic about continuing the exercise, word
after word, until finally the bell rang.

I decided to incorporate this type of imagery exercise into every lesson for about ten minutes. In addition, we practiced *language smoothing,* an activity (described in the episode about Arthur) whereby the subject visualizes various scenes, and simultaneously describes, with my help, the events that he is experiencing.

Note: *Berna's reading rose to a third-grade level by the end of her freshman year. At the end of her sophomore year, she was reading at the fourth-grade level, and her behavior was quite mature.*

A Senior Learns to Read and to Spell

It was during the second semester of Walley's senior year that his English teacher asked me to test him for learning disabilities. He was an intelligent and respectful student, gifted in tennis and track, and obviously came from a caring and supportive family. His tests showed him reading at the first-grade level.

He responded well to Englemann's *Direct Instruction* decoding program (SRA) and made rapid progress in reading. His spelling, however, remained impossible, so I supplemented his lessons with an adaptation of a strategy I had learned from Dr. Cecilia Pollack. (See Appendix pg. 173.)

The Strategy

I asked Walley to close his eyes and to relax by taking a few comfortable breaths. Then I proceeded to spell aloud the word *people*, watching as he wrote each letter in the air. After going through this procedure three times, Walley said he could see the word in his mind. When I asked him to spell it back to me, he recited *p-e-o-p-e-l*. However, instead of correcting him, I touched his right arm and asked, *"Walley, what is the very last letter in the word, on this side?"* (I omitted the words *left* and *right* to avoid possible confusion.)

He correctly answered *e*. Then I realized that he was looking at the image the way an artist would, noticing first the overall shape, and later the details. I emphasized that he should always spell sequentially, one letter after another, and not reach for the last letter before finishing the word.

We installed two or three more words into his mind in this manner, and thereafter I incorporated the procedure into our lessons every day. Each time, I also checked his spelling of the previously learned words. He retained all of the spellings, and after a week or two, he was able to spell words that we had not even worked on!

By the time June graduation approached, Walley's reading was at the fourth-grade level, and he was off to a very promising start. I regretted that he wouldn't be in school another year, but expected that he would continue to make progress on his own. He visited me the following year and presented me with a flower on Senior Flower Day.

The "Hopeless One" Makes Progress

After two semesters of difficult lessons, incorporating both multi-sensory phonics *and* a whole-word approach, Andrew had progressed from a pre-primary to only a first-grade reading level, with great frustration for us both. In addition, he still needed to spell aloud most words before recognizing them.

At the beginning of our second year together, I employed the following strategy:

- I started by having him read lists of three-letter nonsense syllables. My purpose was to discover which letters gave him the most trouble. After recording his errors, I found that the short vowels *e* and *o* were the most difficult.

- Andrew then closed his eyes, relaxed, and visualized himself writing the problem syllables as I dictated the letters. Sometimes he had to write the syllables two or three times before they remained stable. I had him spell each syllable back to me, in order to assure accuracy.

- Next, I asked him to pronounce the first *letter-sound* (not the letter-name) "on this side," (touching his left arm)

- Then I asked for the sound of the *last* letter, touching his right arm, of course.

- Similarly, I touched his chest for the middle (vowel) sound.

- Next, he practiced putting together the sounds, working from the mental image.

- When he felt secure, I had him open his eyes, look at the printed syllables, and read them aloud **without spelling them first**. He did this without any errors.

From then on, he had no difficulty with the short *e* and *o* syllables, and he no longer had to spell words before being able to recognize them.

We worked through all the six forms of syllables in this manner. At the same time, he accumulated a vocabulary of sight words that are necessary for ordinary reading survival. This was accomplished by yet another strategy. I had him draw an outline picture to represent each new word to be learned. Then I arranged the letters of the word, sequentially, on or around the picture. He visualized the pictures together with their letters, and in this way was able to retain the visual image of the words for future reading or spelling.

Note: *I theorize that he could remember (i.e., see the mental image of) pictures, but not written words. Therefore, when a picture registered in his visual memory, the printed word as* part of the picture, *"slid" into the memory along with it. The picture below is an example of this strategy.*

This is an example of using a picture with a word embedded in it to help one remember the spelling. Other techniques, such as repetition or flash cards, do not seem to work well for the learning disabled. If one can make a mental image of the picture, then all he has to do is to look at that image to see how the word is pronounced or spelled when the need arises.

Chapter Four

Language and Speaking Problems

Language Smoothing

Arthur came to my learning disabilities program as a ninth grader, a quiet young man who was cooperative and smiled readily. His decoding (reading) ability was well above grade level, but his comprehension, as measured by oral tests, was well below grade level.

Arthur's striking difficulty was with oral language. He could barely manage to answer simple questions, such as "How are you?" and his mother reported that, even as a little child, he didn't talk much.

When attempting to answer the simplest of academic questions, his face would redden, and he'd be unable to say anything at all, giving the appearance, however, of thinking very hard. On each occasion I would wait a very long time for him to answer before I supplied the word for him. Then he would get a smile of recognition on his face and say, *"Oh, yes!"*

He would also confuse words, saying *under* when he meant *upon*, and *sofa* when he meant *chair*.

I was greatly puzzled. Thinking he needed practice in comprehending oral language, I assigned him to a program in which he listened to a tape and then answered questions in writing.

The program proved to be much too easy for him, although it was quite difficult for some of the other students. Then I tried two separate strategies, each of which showed remarkable results.

Strategy I

I transferred him to a class in which I was using an oral *thinking-skills* program. I would read a statement aloud and then signal to them to echo what I had read. Arthur repeatedly failed to look at my signals and consequently answered too soon most of the time.

I asked him to look at me when I was speaking, and when he spoke to me. He cooperated, but became red in the face each time. He acknowledged feeling uncomfortable,

Thereupon, I used the principle of *paradoxical intention* by asking him to experience his discomfort deliberately. I told him I **wanted** him to feel uncomfortable; he was **supposed** to feel as embarrassed as he possibly could. After that, his discomfort apparently disappeared, and he ceased getting red. From then on, I had no difficulty getting him to respond in unison with the rest of the class. Apparently my giving him permission to feel embarrassed, and even to exaggerate his discomfort, had the effect of freeing him.

Strategy II

Here I adapted Win Wenger's *Language Smoothing* strategy (pg viii). I had Arthur close his eyes and see himself standing in front of a door. Then I told him to describe the door aloud. He used one or two words in answer to my specific questions, volunteering no information on his own. When I asked him to open the door and tell me where he was, he answered, *"My house,"* sounding surprised that I didn't know.

As he described his bedroom in one- or two-word answers to my questions, I constructed full sentences with the information and asked him to repeat the sentences. For example, when I asked him what he was looking at, he replied *bed*. Then I would say, *"I'm looking at my bed"* and he would echo my words. (I theorize that by speaking words to describe the scene in his mind as he watched it, he was causing connections to develop or strengthen between the imaging and the speech areas of his brain.) I then would say, *"Wasn't that easy?"* to which he would smilingly answer, *"Yes."* (Eyes still closed and viewing his scene.)

We continued this imaging exercise, describing other things in the room in a similar manner. On succeeding days, we visited different rooms of his house.

Part of My Therapy Plan for Arthur

1. Ask him a question upon his arrival in class each day. The purpose is to force him to mentally *see* the answer to my question. Then, while looking at the image, he should be able to answer me correctly.

Sample questions:
How many rooms are there in your house?
What color is your mother's hair?
How many chairs are in your kitchen?

How many sisters do you have?
How many brothers do you have?
How many children does your mother have?
What color is your bedroom wallpaper?

2. Before the formal part of the lesson begins, have him see a golden light filling his brain and extending through to his ears. Suggest that the light keeps him wide awake and makes it easy to understand what the teacher is saying. He is to see himself with his mouth closed while he listens.

What follows are examples of the kinds of oral answers that Arthur gave to my questions.

Arthur, how many rooms are there in your apartment?
"Three."
Please name them and show me the numbers on your fingers.
"Living room" (one finger) *"and three bedrooms."* (two fingers)
When you said three bedrooms, you showed only two fingers. (Arthur corrects it with some resistance.)
Arthur, how many rooms is that?
"Four."
Don't you have any other rooms?
"Living room, three bedrooms, and bathroom. Five."
(The number of fingers he displays does not match the number of rooms that he names, so I help him to correct his finger-voice coordination.)
Arthur, are you sure that's all there are?
"Yeah." (almost indignantly)
Where does your mother cook?
"Kitchen. Oh, yeah." (Counts)

Perhaps he didn't spontaneously see a mental image in response to my spoken words. Most people, when asked how many rooms are in their house, would automatically visualize each room as they counted them.

I didn't realize how much the exercises had helped Arthur until I encountered him in the hall the following week, holding an art folder under his arm.

Hi, Arthur! Did you bring some drawings to school, as you promised?

"*Oh no, these are Jimmy's. I'm holding them for him while he's making a phone call.*"

Arthur! You're talking in full sentences!!

"*I know,*" *he smiled.*

I asked if he was talking a lot more at home also, and he replied that he was.

I immediately called the reading consultant who made time to retest Arthur then and there. A short time later she phoned me. *"What did you do to him?"* she demanded incredulously. His scores were *off the charts.*

Arthur's mother was so happy that she brought me a lovely pen and pencil set.

Comment

Somewhere in the process of attempting to transform a thought into spoken words, Arthur apparently would forget what he wanted to say. In other words, the initial thought disappeared when he tried to convert it into speech. It was as though the pathways between the thought and speech areas of his brain were too weak to successfully transport the thought over into speech. Consequently he found it difficult or impossible to answer most questions orally. On the other hand, when he attempted to translate a thought into *written* language, the thought did *not* disappear. Evidently the pathways from thought to hand were intact. Using this metaphor, I theorized that Arthur needed to strengthen the connections ("pathways") between the thought and speech areas of his brain. I enabled him to accomplish this by having him visualize his thoughts (i.e., turn them into mental pictures) and simultaneously echo sentences that described his mental pictures. Thus, connections developed and his oral answers became easy and smooth.

Arthur's Feedback—Answers to Essay Questions

> *I Learn Everything in Mrs Gifford class. I Learn how to read and write and how to understand what had been taught in class and also I Lean to participate in class and to keep my mouth closed when a teacher is talking in class.*
>
> *I Like Mrs. Gifford class because it helps me to understand Everything in her class and it helps me to Respect another student and Learn to do the work and Learn to spell each word and say it.*
>
> *I would not like to change this class because this class helps me to do my work and to spell the word and say it and also it helps me to listen what the teacher have to say and it also helps me to close my eyes and to see the golden sunlight so that I would understand Everything and be wide awake when a teacher is talking in class.*

Bilingual *and* Language Disabled

In my first year as a teacher, I was seeing students one on one, and Juan was one of my first pupils. He was a friendly, good-natured ninth-grader who had great difficulty express-ing himself. In addition to speaking rapidly and indistinctly, his grammar and vocabulary were so confused that even were I to grasp the words, I still could get the wrong idea. For example, he would say *he* for *she* and *up* for *down*, etc.

The following outline describes one of the first strategies that I used with him:

1. *I asked him to slow his speech while I wrote, word for word, the things he was saying.*

2. *Next, having his words visually in front of me, I could figure out what he meant and then reword the message into intelligible English.*

3. *He would read back my corrected version, meanwhile slowing down and articulating the words according to my instructions.*

4. *He would practice this until he could say the message comfortably without having to rely upon the written words. This procedure worked well, and over time his language improved greatly.*

In his senior year, he announced that he had won a scholar-ship to study ballet at an arts academy in Litchfield. Try-outs had been held at the San Juan Center where he had been going for help with homework, *"and they found out I could move."* I was thrilled for him.

He studied ballet with them for two years, performing at

the Bushnell Memorial and on television. He met famous dancers and entertainers, mentioning ZsaZsa Gabor among others. He grew from a naive inner-city kid to a more sophisticated young man, learning to eat brown rice, tofu, and yogurt. Equally interesting, his language was enormously improved.

A couple of years after he graduated he came to visit me at school, bringing me a box of cookies. I remember his saying, as we walked out of school together, *Life is very hard when you have a learning disability.*

Despite this reality, he managed to get hired by the Public Library. He worked in the periodicals room, and on Saturday mornings he would read stories to the children. He acknowledged that he felt apprehensive when he had to read, but he evidently did a fine job. They gave him promotions and raises, and he saved enough money to buy a three-family house for members of his family, and a single home for himself.

Our teacher-student relationship blossomed into a friendship. He is no longer an adolescent kid, but has grown to be an intelligent and fine man.

A Lesson in Communication

Estel and Margaret came into class, yelling angrily at each other. I couldn't understand what they were saying as they tried to tell me what had happened. Their explanations were a jumble of "she's," while talking about several different girls. Finally I decided to exploit the situation as a lesson in clear communication. That is, I would model unambiguous, sequential speaking.

Since I did not want to turn it into a lesson of gossiping

about others, I had them use names like *the small girl* and *the big girl*, etc., to represent the absent persons. The terms *she* and *he* were not permitted, because of the ambiguity they caused. As they spoke, I outlined the account on the chalkboard, rearranging their random statements into a sequential order.

Two students objected to the use of class time on someone's "personal business." They said we should be spending our time on reading.

I reminded them that, before having success in reading, it is necessary to be able to listen carefully and to understand spoken language, as well as to speak clearly. I reminded them that we had spent much time learning about sequencing and its importance in reading and spelling. As regards "personal business," the girls had brought their business into class, and as long as they were willing, it was more useful to teach from real life situations than from a lesson in a book.

There were no further complaints, and we continued, with no problem of maintaining interest and attention.

After the bell signaled the end of the class period, two boys remained behind to comment favorably upon the lesson.

Past Tense Dilemma

John decoded (could read words) on a higher level than his classmates, but when it came to thinking, he was abnormally rigid and conventional. He would speak of joining the army upon graduation, and I visualized him saluting stiffly in his uniform.

During one lesson, it became apparent that he didn't understand the term *past tense* or the meaning of the *ed* suffix.

It seemed also that he barely understood the meanings of the words *present* and *future*. I hit upon the following strategy:

1. *I ask him to sit upright at his desk, eyes closed.*
"Feel the wooden seat beneath you; feel your feet on the floor."

2. *I touch his chest midline and say, "See yourself sitting here." He nods.*

3. *"Now see yourself at home yesterday and point to the direction where you see the picture of yesterday." He points to his left.*

4. *"Now see yourself at home tomorrow. Point to where you see that scene." He points to his right.*

5. *"Good. Now put a square frame around each of those pictures." He nods.*

6. *"Now open your eyes."*

7. *On the chalkboard I draw three contiguous squares in a horizontal direction. I write the words,* **Now** *above the center square,* **Yesterday** *above the left square, and* **Tomorrow** *above the right square.*

8. *"Look at the words above the squares. Now please close your eyes and let me know when you see these three words written above the squares like here on the board." (If student has trouble visualizing the words, have him write them mentally, as you dictate the spelling for each word, two or three times.) After he indicates that he sees the words above the squares, I have him recite them to me, eyes still closed. He does so.*

9. *He looks at the board again, as I add the following*

Learning the Meanings of
Past, Present, Future

Students study the chart below until they can reproduce it correctly from memory.

Yesterday	Now	Tomorrow
Past	**Present**	**Future**
-ed		**will-**

The blank chart below is used to test students.

Directions:
1) Write the following words in the correct boxes at the top of the chart: **Now, Yesterday, Tomorrow**
2) Next, write these words in the correct boxes: **Future, Past, Present**
3) Below that, write the ending **-ED**, and the word **WILL** in *their* correct boxes.

words: **Present** *(below* Now*);*   **Past** *(below* Yesterday*) ;*
Future *(below* Tomorrow*).*

10. *"Now close your eyes and add these three words to your mental image, like on the board." The process is verified as above.*

11. *We continue adding to the chart in the same manner. Inside the left square, (labeled* Past*) I have him install the letters* **ed**. *Inside the right square (labeled* Future*) he installs the word* **will**.

12. *When he has done this, I ask him to repeat back to me what he sees in his mind, and he says in staccato tones:*
> "Present"—*pointing directly in front of himself;*
> "Past"—*pointing to his left;*
> "Future"—*pointing to his right.*

13. *I ask him to open his eyes and draw on the board the squares and words he has imaged. After this, he had no trouble with tenses. Whenever the subject came up, he would close his eyes, point stiffly in the three directions, and say in the staccato voice, "Past, Present, Future."*

Mariela Writes a Letter to Her Stepfather

I often found it impossible to understand what Mariela was saying, because her English was so poor. One strategy that helped was the same one I had used with several other students: namely, writing down her words, figuring out her meaning, and then rewording the message in simple English by writing my version beneath hers. She would then read my sentences aloud, until she could recite them from memory.

Believing that one can learn skills more readily if the content of the lesson is important to the learner, I listened to her most recent complaint about the way her step-father treated her. I suggested she write a letter to let him know how she feels, since she is unable to be effective when she talks in person. I advised her to dictate the letter to me, and I would see if I could understand what she was trying to say.

She agreed to try it. As she spoke, I wrote down her words with a little coaching here and there. Then she copied my sentences in her own handwriting. The letter follows:

Dear Alvardo,

Why you mad at me? I feel scared when you look at me wrong. Why you don't like my boyfriend? He act like a gentle man and treat me with respect. We only talk and kiss sometime. He never touch me private. I love him a lot.

Are you jealous? You should not boss me because you are not my real father. My mother should tell me what to do. It is not your problem. Please respect me, and I can respect you.

The following day Mariela reported that he had read the letter and then knocked on her door and apologized.

Mariela's Feedback

1. What did you learn in this class this year?

I learn in your class aeiou and I read them much better In your class and I learn much better in your class. I love to stay in you class bicouse you are a nice teacher you help me alot with my pralms [problems] that I have in my house. I Love you.

2. What did you like about this class?

I like to learn much better in your class bicouse I don't know how to rite English and you teach me how to rite English. I hope you has a nice sammer vacation with your huspen.
I Love you.

3. What would you like to change about this class?

I like to change [myself so] that wen you talk I can't talk.
I Love you.

Section Two

Vignettes: Student

Attitudes and

Behaviors

Chapter Five

The Experience of Being Learning Disabled

Processing New Students

As part of my diagnostic and information-gathering procedures, I ask newly arrived students to write the alphabet and the months of the year, along with their names, addresses, schedules, etc. My reason is that, since most learning disabled people have difficulty with sequencing, the alphabet and months are problematic for them.

I had learned that it's necessary explain to the students ahead of time the meaning and importance of the concept of sequencing. Otherwise, the students are offended by my asking them to do what they regard as "baby work".

I usually begin by telling them what I believe the term *Learning Disability* really means and what it's like to be a learning disabled student. The class listens intently and afterwards willingly complies with my request that they write the alphabet, etc. My account to the students follows on the next page.

Discussion of the Term Learning Disability

Most teachers know only one way to teach: they talk and students listen. If you happen to be a person who enjoys language, you have a good chance of doing well in school. If, on the other hand, you enjoy other things, but not language, you may be called "learning disabled."

For example, you might be good at art, music or science; or at sports, building things, or fixing cars; but if language is hard for you, they might call you "learning disabled."

In the present system, as long as students are good with language, no one calls them "learning disabled," even if they can't do any of those other things. No one insults them with that label.

But what people forget is that the world needs many different kinds of talents. Most people are good at some things and not at others. When we appreciate each person for being herself or himself, we can be respectful and not call anyone "learning disabled."

*Some day the colleges will train teachers how to teach **all** students, not just the ones whose talent is language. Teachers will learn to use music and rhythm, stories and games, and the imagination. The students will be able to learn in a natural way, and **all** the kids will learn.*

Then I explain that sequencing is one of the skills needed for reading and writing, and for reciting the alphabet, etc. .

I explain that sequencing means the ability to talk and to think in an orderly manner, and I demonstrate by writing the alphabet in and out of sequence.When I then describe the experience of being an LD student in school, the class listens with intense interest.

What It's Like to Be an LD Kid in School
A Brief Story

Imagine a four-year-old child at home, happily playing and helping his mother. The family thinks he is a smart little boy—until he turns five and has to go to school.

There he is in kindergarten, and the teacher is talking and talking; but the poor little kid doesn't know what she's talking about half the time, because language isn't his thing. But everyone seems to be having a good time talking, so he talks, too, even when it has nothing to do with what the teacher is saying. The teacher doesn't like that and tells him to be quiet. The little child feels bad.

In first grade, the teacher makes strange marks on the board and tells the children to copy them. The boy doesn't understand the marks, because they have no relationship to his world. They belong to the world of language; and remember, language is something to which he pays little attention. So he just makes funny marks on his paper, like he thinks the other children are doing. But the teacher tells him he's doing it wrong. He feels very bad and wonders if he's dumb. He tries extra hard and is afraid to write anything unless the teacher is right next to him, to make sure he does it correctly.

In the following grades, he really worries that maybe he is retarded or crazy. He decides that no one must know that he can't read or write. Maybe he decides to be a clown so they won't realize the truth. Or maybe he starts to be a trouble-maker—anything to hide the truth. He'd rather be sent to the principal's office and be punished than admit he can't read or write. Some children might decide to sit at the back of the room and be very quiet so that the teacher will not notice them. Then the teacher thinks, "he's a nice boy," and passes him because he tries hard.

And so it goes until middle school, when he might turn to stealing, or drugs, etc., because he's so frustrated. Or he might just keep on trying his best and being scared, and somehow making it through school just by staying out of trouble. In any case, it's not fair.

The students relate to the story and appear to feel validated and relieved, at least for the moment.

Chapter Six

"Hopeless" Students

Elwood's Story

After teaching for almost twenty-one years, I still encountered student behaviors I'd not seen before. A particularly difficult case was Elwood. When he entered ninth grade, he was unable to read on the first-grade level. His eighth-grade teacher had advised him to buy a little electronic device into which he could punch the letters of an unknown word, and a voice would pronounce the word for him. It was thus that he attended my reading classes, with his electronic reader periodically saying words aloud during the individual "seat work" part of the lesson. I banished the gadget from class, explaining to Elwood that he was to learn word-attack skills instead.

Another entry behavior was his habit of keeping his eyelids half-closed and responding to questions with either a shrug or a brief indistinct answer, often unrelated to the question that was asked. He was of bulky build and walked and moved at a slow, tired pace. When seated, he would lean his head on his hand or rest it on the desk. Consequently, before I got to know him, he impressed me as being a sluggish, slow-witted, uninteresting (perhaps hopeless?) student. He told me that whenever he came to a new school, he would get into fights and apparently was helpless to understand and correct the situation.

It soon became apparent, however, that far from being less intelligent than the other students, he was probably brighter. In science class, I would teach by lecture-discussions, omitting the need for them to read the book. At such times, he understood and remembered the material better than the other students did. When we used the book, it would be read orally, so that Elwood and several others could benefit.

I realized that it would be easier for me to teach him if he didn't look half-asleep all the time. I, therefore, looked for rare instances when his eyes were open, and I immediately would compliment him: *"Elwood, you look so wide awake. Your eyes are wide open!"* He received extra points every time I caught him like this. Within a short time, Elwood's eyes were open all the time in my classes.

Once, as I handed him a worksheet, he responded with his customary groan, making a smart-aleck, put-down remark. I suddenly realized that Elwood was merely trying to sound sophisticated!

"Do you know how I feel when you say those things?" I asked him. He answered that he didn't know, so I told him that I felt insulted and angry. He was genuinely surprised and never did it again.

One day, at the end of class, Roger angrily said he was going to punch Elwood. I asked what had made him so angry, since I hadn't seen Elwood do anything wrong. Roger replied that whenever he is talking to someone, Elwood always "has something to say." In other words, Elwood made insulting remarks during someone else's conversation. I realized what was happening: Elwood wanted to feel like "one of the guys", so he would make what he thought were sophisticated "smart" comments. The trouble is that he didn't know his remarks were insulting and unwelcome. He just didn't understand the banter of the boys.

I explained this to Roger, and he indicated that he understood. He agreed to try to help me teach Elwood how to speak more appropriately.

When next I saw Elwood, I repeated the conversation I'd had with Roger. I explained that, while he (Elwood) was smarter than many kids, when it came to joking around, he just didn't have that kind of a mind. Instead of trying to sound cool, he should just be himself. He understood my point, especially when I mentioned that this kind of wisecrack could well explain why he had so much trouble with kids wanting to fight him.

Elwood has gifts and intelligence that are superior to many students. One time, I wanted to arrange four desks close together so that they would form a square. It would make for closer interaction, like sitting around a table. I didn't know how to arrange them so that no one would have to climb over the bar that attached each seat to its desk. When the students entered, I gave them the task of arranging the desks, and Elwood was the only person who could do it. It was apparent that he could visualize the placement of the desks beforehand.

Toward the end of the school year, I became aware, for the first time, of the habitual look in Elwood's eyes when he entered the classroom. He would walk into the room with his eyes unfocused. Until then, I had just accepted it as "Elwood", but this time I recognized that this was his way of protecting himself, so that others would not be able to tell what he was feeling. He had once explained that he keeps his face expressionless when he is attacked by anyone. [In his book *Psycheye (1977)* Ahsen cites a similar experience. His patient visualized and reported an incident from a childhood, in which he never smiled. Later he said *"...the most astounding (images) were of the boy (himself) who was constantly picked on by the other boys at the place ...I was surprised to see in one image that there was life within this boy*].

I role-played the scene for Elwood, copying his way of keeping his eyes unfocused while entering my classroom. Then I replayed it, but this time I walked in with focused eyes and a friendly hello. He indicated that he understood. It was the end of the school year by then, so I didn't have a chance until the following fall to discover that he did indeed alter his behavior.

When it came to academics, I was able to use imagery to help Elwood learn the sounds of the letters. He learned so well that he became the most phonics-knowledgeable student in the class, and in fact was able to help the student teacher (who was himself learning disabled). However, Elwood was still faced with the overwhelming task of blending the individual sounds into words, and for this problem I used not only imagery, but also the *Blend-It* program that was created by Cecilia Pollack (Book-Lab). By the end of his freshman year, Elwood had achieved the first-grade reading level. While this may seem to the reader to be hopelessly slow progress, I think that a strong beginning was made. Sometimes, when reading aloud to me, he would say, *"I know the word, but I just can't get it out."*

I told him that perhaps he needed to make stronger connections among the areas of his brain, especially between the thought and speech areas. The easiest way I knew to accomplish this was for him to see mental images and simultaneously describe what he was seeing (Wenger, 1976). He refused to do this, although he would comply when asked to write words in his mind. It's evident that he was afraid to visualize scenes, undoubtedly because he feared painful feelings from his past. Perhaps if I had asked him to describe a specific room, instead of a "scene", he would have found it less threatening. (See section on *Language Smoothing*, Chapter Six.)

At the beginning of the semester, I had asked the students to write a paragraph about their vision of a *Perfect World*. Elwood handed in his paper with two words written on it: *No world*. Later, he told me that he'd first started feeling bad about everything when he was in the third or fourth grade. He claimed that his teachers in kindergarten, first, and second grade had refused to teach him how to read.

At the end of the school year, however, when the students wrote their memories of the past year's classroom events, Elwood's paper was most rewarding for me. It appears at the end of the Elwood story.

Elwood's Drawing

I asked the students to draw a picture of themselves as a change of pace from their academics. Elwood made a puzzling picture, and I asked Stan to interpret it. Stan was a fellow student who drew exceptionally well. He made the following comments:

Feels trapped.
Thinks in a different direction.
Trying to get out of the block.

Elwood's drawing.

There's a mirror image in the center: like he's looking at himself. It's a closed door that he hasn't opened yet.

In light of the above interpretation of Elwood's drawing, as well as my experiences with him that year, I had hopes that Elwood would eventually open the door to see himself and get out of his block. He already had shown remarkable growth since I had given him feedback about the effect of his remarks upon other people. The *Feedback* part of his final exam revealed that he had, indeed, gained some valuable understanding of his own behavior. I believed he could mature into a happier young man who would be freed to share his talents and intelligence with others.

Note: The following September, after I retired, I had occasion to visit the school and encountered Elwood in the corridor. I was pleased at the change in his appearance: not only did he look slimmer, but his eyes had a clearer and more present quality than they had had the previous June. I hope he has continued to mature in this direction.

Feedback from Elwood (as he read it to me from his paper)

Lrn [we learned] *about Reading and your self. let me tell you about the year. In* [fall] *1993 I cane in to this clasroon I sat down. I met a kid name khalid we were stating* (starting) *trubl in the clasroon. we were boting* [bothering] *the stundent teetr when she was teeting. Unther* [another] *day was had* [hard] *khalid was Ranking on me and I was getting in to fights and skipping. I was stating* [starting] *to slow down* [from the bad stuff] *and pay attention in mae* [my] *clas. by*

November I was learming better in me [my] *clas.*

In the year 1994 [second semester, same year] *I cool down a lot in me.* [In] *nod* [mod] *1 ther were 14 kids in the begining of the year in this roon now ther are only 3 kids. I am learning to Read more and makeing more fres* [friends] *in school. You as* [ask] *me wut I lear*[n] *in this clas ther this year. I lear*[n] *about being ne self* [myself] *don't act lick* [like] *a big shot or a clas clwn* [clown]. *this is my story this is for Real.*

P.S. Ms. Gifford
I see you wen I see you. This is Elwood Jr 9 greater [9th grader] *signing off.*
The end of the school year
June 17

Corman Learns to Visualize

Corman made no progress in reading during the first six months that he was in my ninth-grade class. He usually couldn't concentrate on my questions or instructions, no matter how simple they were. In fact, an observer would have thought he didn't understand English, although when students spoke to him he responded normally.

When he did reply sensibly to me, he very much needed to feel that he was right. He would sometimes say, *"Oh, I know; you're trying to make me say* (such and such)," indicating that I couldn't trick him.

Reading and grammar rules fell upon deaf ears, not because he was incapable of understanding them, but rather because his mind was closed, and normal instruction could not get past the barrier. Consequently, instead of rules, I tried installing images in his mind. Again I was frustrated; he said that he couldn't see the images. Feeling almost hopeless, I gave up trying imagery with him.

One time, when I realized that he didn't understand the terms *past* and *future*, I made a chart illustrating the three tenses. He memorized it and tested himself every day. It took only one or two trials for him to write the chart correctly and, consequently, to understand the terms. (see a copy of the chart on page 36 in *Past Tense Dilemma*.)

The imagery break-through finally occurred one day, after he couldn't read the simple word "when". Without telling him the word, I wrote it on the chalkboard and then told him to take the chalk and trace on my letters, spelling aloud as he wrote. Next, he was to write the letters on the board, keeping his eyes closed and again spelling aloud as he wrote. After a few confused attempts, he finally followed the instructions successfully. Then he opened his eyes, looked at the word on the board, and said "when," having first seen and recognized it in his mind.

We repeated this strategy with several more words, until he relaxed enough to realize that he was visualizing them. A few days later, I was astonished to see him not only paying attention to the lesson but also closing his eyes and visualizing, All this he was doing on his own, without any reminders from me.

Shortly afterward, I retested his reading ability and found that his score had risen two levels—from a second- to a fourth-grade level. His behavior continued to be cooperative.

The following school year, to my disappointment, however, Corman attended school usually not more than three or four days a week. When he did come, he would sit quietly, but fail to concentrate, even for one minute at a time.

During the first half of the year, it was impossible to teach him anything. Since he was on the track team, I tried to contact the coach for some input or collaboration but got no response. When I asked Corman if he was on drugs, he would laugh and shake his head but say nothing.

He expressed resentment if I asked him anything he considered not my business. Finally, I wrote him a note:

Dear Corman,

I'm writing instead of talking, because you don't listen when I talk. I do not care what you do in your private life. I tried to help you learn to read better, but if you don't care enough to help yourself, then there is nothing I can do about it.

From now on, you don't have to worry that I will bother you in class. I realize that you do not want my help this year. You know that without my help, you will not keep your attention on what I am explaining. I hate to see you fail this course, but it seems there is nothing I can do about it.

Good luck anyway.

Mildred Gifford

After receiving this note, Corman's attitude became much more cooperative, although his attendance didn't improve. During the second half of the year, I often worked with him during my planning time. On one occasion I discovered that he didn't understand how to draw a two-dimensional floor plan. He would try to include the upright walls, which of course was impossible. Explanations, accompanied by my drawings, did not help. Finally I placed two open cartons side by side and had him look inside. I told him to notice only the horizontal "floors" divided by a line representing the vertical walls. After that, he drew a reasonable floor plan of his apartment and was even able to describe it to me with his eyes closed, a formerly impossible task.

"What does all that have to do with reading?" some may ask. I have learned that the more easily one can visualize abstract images such as symbols and floor plans, the better are the chances for success in reading, speaking, and thinking in general. (See *Language Smoothing.*)

In the hope of helping him to relax, I taught him to meditate by closing his eyes and listening to sounds both within and outside himself, or he could meditate by paying attention to his feelings. He was to silently name them, such as *angry* and *scared*, and to deliberately stay with those feelings for twenty minutes. I find that when students do this, they experience relief.

Although I didn't find the time to check his progress on these assignments (I doubt that he practiced daily), he later told me that he did find peace and calm by listening to a classical music tape I had given him.

Corman was quite upset when I told him I was going to retire. He said, "I think you should wait two, three more years." He had evidently come to depend upon me for more than just academic support. I had mixed feelings about this: I was glad our relationship helped to relieve, to some extent, his hopeless feelings, but I knew that I couldn't always be there. I assured him we could stay in touch and, indeed, he has phoned me frequently since my retirement. After the first day of school the following September, he called to say he had stayed home, because, having just received his report card in the mail, he learned he had not been promoted. He blamed orthodontist appointments for his absences, and I pointed out that, regardless of the reasons, if he was absent during lessons, he couldn't learn the subject, and failing to learn is just what *F* means.

He admitted that he was ashamed to go to school, because he had stayed back, so I reminded him that tomorrow he could visualize himself surrounded by a protective white light. He had used this strategy for protection when walking home from track practice late in the day. He then agreed to go to school and later phoned to acknowledge that it wasn't so bad.

Because he loves flowers, I had encouraged him to join a group to help beautify the school grounds. I'm hoping that this kind of extra-curricular activity, plus his interest in religion, will strengthen his morale and help him feel a little more confident about himself.

That same year following my retirement, one of his teachers told me that he was responding well to her strict demands for homework. He obviously appreciated her strong disciplinary attitude.

Feedback from Corman

April 13 [freshman year]

My name is Corman R and I ben doing a lot of imagery with Miss Gifford. it hlep [help] *win you need to focus yory* [your] *mind. I like to run track and imagery hlep me to focus you can see tinking in yory mind that* [when] *you have thoth* [thoughts] *you couldn't see but sometime it is a litte* [little] *bleree. but you can still see it. imagery is a good exsorsize I tink poelpe* [people] *shood use it.*

Eric's Story:
Phobic about *"Special Ed"*

It was already May of his freshman year when Eric first came to my reading class. He refused to allow me to test him, and the following day when I happened to mention the term *special ed*, he exclaimed, "Is this a special ed class?" I answered that it was, and he immediately asked to see his counselor. After that, I didn't see him again until almost the end of the school year, when the head teacher told him he'd be expelled if he cut any more classes.

When he finally returned to my class, he sat down and immediately began belittling me and the work we were doing. He interrupted my analysis of the *Phonovisual Chart* (an excellent chart that helps students to understand and remember the correct pronunciation of the consonants). When he told me I was wrong, I invited him to point out my error and to teach the lesson. He came to the front of the room and postured as though ready to speak. When no one said anything, he shook his head and sat down, saying he understood it but couldn't explain it.

The following year Eric didn't come to class until February. Then, after attending for a few days, he came in and asked to see the school social worker. Since the social worker was unavailable and Eric seemed upset, I decided to speak with him myself. I put the class into their "peer tutoring" mode, with Torrie (one of the students) conducting the lesson by reading aloud from the *Direct Instruction* program. Eric and I sat in the back of the room, talking quietly.

I asked him to describe the scene that had upset him, and it soon became apparent that he has been upset since at least the eighth grade. That was when he was first placed into a special program for emotionally disturbed students. Eric traced all his trouble to that event and was consumed with regrets that he didn't straighten up at the time.

I said, "*I believe everyone has within themselves the answers to their own problems, but they often don't know it, because they are busy repressing painful thoughts. The trouble with repressing one part of your mind is that other parts become repressed also, and that can include your own wisdom.*" I invited him to try some imagery to get in touch with this part, and he agreed to try.

He said he was worried because he had cut some classes the day before. He described intensely anxious feelings, such as headache, chest tightness, nausea, and strange feelings in the arms.

As he continued, it became clear that he was worried about more than just the episode of the previous day. Every scene he described revealed anxiety that stemmed from a **previous** experience. At this point, it seemed that we could be involved in a hopeless regression. Therefore, instead of envisioning past events, I decided to switch to visiting his *Wise Being*.

When I suggested that he see himself in a beautiful place, he readily volunteered that he was on a deserted beach, lying on the hot sand, with blue sky above and sparkling ocean nearby. I directed his attention to a fluffy cloud floating gently toward him. A peaceful smile appeared on his face. I had the cloud settle around him and softly transport him to his castle on the distant mountain. He went in and saw his own Wise Being awaiting him. I told him that the Wise Being was very happy to see him and greeted him with love and joy.

I instructed him to tell the Being his problem. I then said that the Wise One was giving him something, and Eric nodded. After they said good-bye, the cloud carried him back to the beach. In response to my question, he said he still had the gift, and that it was a golden key. (Earlier I had said the Wise Being would give him a gift that would be a key to his problem, and immediately realized I had used too specific a word by saying *"key."*)

At this point, unfortunately, the bell rang. Eric opened his eyes, bewildered as to where he was. I reminded him that he was in reading class, and we had done some imagery. He remarked that he felt very peaceful and seemed to forget that he had asked to see the social worker. I told Eric to be certain to come back to see me during my planning time.

When he returned, he said, *"I want to thank you for what you did. I feel so much better now."*

I responded by asking about the golden key. He stared at me, saying, *"Are you all right?"*

"Of course," I replied, realizing that he had no memory of the imagery.

"Are you sure you're all right?" he asked, backing away almost imperceptibly.

At this point I assured him that we were both fine, and that he had gone so deeply into the imagery that when the bell rang, he forgot the experience, just as one forgets a dream if awakened suddenly. I suggested that, having been so anxious before, it may have been a relief to have trusted me and to have let go of his tensions. Having mentioned the key, I felt I had to explain, and I briefly recounted his story.

He listened with interest, saying, *"I wonder what that golden key was about."* When he couldn't come up with an idea, I suggested that perhaps the key was to unlock the courage in his heart. When he felt anxious and frightened, his heart's courage could fill him and surround him like a protective light. He said he understood, and agreed to try it.

Knowing that Eric played the piano and sang in a choir, I asked who his favorite composers were. When he replied *"Mozart"* and *"Beethoven"*, I suggested that this kind of music could be very relaxing when he was feeling nervous or upset. He said he would try listening to CD's at such times.

Eric has appeared to be calm since then. Recently he told me that whenever he feels upset, he listens to the music and drifts blissfully into imagery. He added that he told his mother about the therapeutic effect of the music, and that now she, too, relaxes by listening to her CD's when she feels distressed.

Eric's Feedback

Well, I was not here for the full year but when I come to this class I really enjoyed myself Ms. Gifford you helped me a hole lot you helped me threw the good time as well as the bad time. and I thank you for all the help you give me. because there are not a lot of teacher how [who] *would have help the way you did. you help* [me] *to be able to relast* [relax] *when I'm reading and that help me a lot.*

Well I really don't remember any activities because I was not here half of the time but I learned a hole lot.

Well, I would have change my attitude toward the classss[classes] *becouse I did not want to be in any of the classss I'm in now.*

Chapter Seven

Disrespectful and Uncooperative Behavior

Music Hath Charms

One morning, only Susan and Karla showed up for my first period class. They were obviously feeling out of sorts. Each sat down silently and looked away from the other. There was no response to my friendly "good morning".

I realized that attempting to get them to communicate with each other or to attend to a lesson was going to be unsuccessful. I decided, therefore, not to bother trying to teach to closed ears. Instead, I put a tape of light-hearted music on the audio-cassette player. (*Raindrops Keep Falling on My Head*, by the Baroque Connection.)

Within a very short time, Susan, who had her head down on the desk, raised her head with a pleasant expression on her face and opened her folder.

I began the lesson, and Karla joined in with the responses. The atmosphere lightened and we had a fruitful lesson.

Test the Teacher—Randy

This is one of my favorite stories. It was my second year of teaching, and my classes were very cozy, with five kids fitting into a very small office containing a table for them and a desk for me.

We were part way through the school year, when Randy began a habit of entering the room exactly while the bell was ringing, rather than before, which would have been the normal pattern. I ignored the behavior.

Then he began to enter the room at the instant the bell *stopped* ringing. It was apparent to me that he was testing to see how far he could go before I said anything.

Having recently read *Games People Play*, by Eric Berne, M.D. (1964), I was prepared to deal with this obvious game. After he entered just barely late a couple of times, I recognized that he was daring me to give him a detention. Then he could be "justifiably offended," having been barely a second late.

I said to him, "Randy, there's a book called *Games People Play*, and it describes a game called, 'Now I've Got You, You Son-Of-A-Bitch!'" Smiling at Randy's shock at my use of such a term, I continued. "You're playing a slightly different version of that game. You want to push me until I give you a detention. Then you can indicate how bad *I* am with the message 'Now *You've* Got *Me*, You Son-Of-A-Bitch!'"

A grin of recognition crossed Randy's face. He said nothing, but never played his game again. The episode, however, had an even more delightful and unexpected ending. After the interchange, Randy became a loyal and enthusiastic student, showing a great deal of progress academically. The class periods were too short for his satisfaction, and he achieved an A+ average.

Teasing Classmates—Henry

Henry's story is one of those successes that we wish could happen to all of our students. A tall, nice-looking sophomore, he was referred to me by his counselor, who felt there had to be a reason why this alert young man could read at only the first-grade level.

I diagnosed him as "learning disabled," and he was scheduled into my class. This was early in my career, before I had encountered the magic of imagery, or even a program called *Direct Instruction.*(This is a carefully-sequenced, phonics-based reading program.) I include this anecdote and the previous two as examples of applying the *Aikido* attitude, described in Chapter Ten.

Much as I enjoyed having him as a student—he caught on quickly and applied what he learned—he had a habit of teasing that, although meant in humor, was hurtful to other people. The problem was that he jokingly insulted Mike and Bob, two of the other students. These two boys had difficulties beyond just reading and spelling. They didn't understand Henry's humor and often misunderstood people's intentions.

Henry would refer to the two boys as "el blancos." They were the only "white" students in the group, the others being Puerto Rican or African-American. He would ridicule them in a kidding manner. Mike always got angry, and soon Bob took to copying Henry and also started to ridicule Mike. When I scolded Bob, he would say, "But I was only kidding. Can't he even take a joke?"

Nothing I said to Henry made an impression strong enough to end the hurtful habit. I tried role-playing, lecturing, and reasoning. I refrained from giving a detention because I wanted to avoid a power struggle, feeling instinctively that forcing him in this manner would do nothing to enlighten Henry's attitude.

Then one day I had an inspiration. When the students came into the room, I wrote the following word on the board: "BULLY." Then I asked Henry if he could read the word. He immediately became gloomy and remained silent for the remainder of the period, refusing to participate in the lesson. I realized he understood the message and was insulted.

The Happy Ending is that from that time forward, Henry stopped expressing humor through insults.

The Further Happy Ending is that by the time he graduated, he was reading on the tenth-grade level, having responded well to an Orton-Gillingham method of instruction. When he graduated, he gave me a picture of himself. On the back he had written, "To my best teacher."

I felt like a million.

Disruptive, Immature Behavior—Mitchel

Mitchel's behavior and speech intonations reminded me of a seven-year-old, although he was more capable academically than his peers. I was stumped as to how to help him feel and behave in a more age-appropriate manner.

One morning before school, I encountered him in the hallway. "What are you doing in the hall before the bell?" I asked.

He replied, "I think I'm on inside suspension. I have to see Mrs. T."

An idea occurred to me, and, having ample time, I decided to try it. "Mitchel, you look to me like you don't feel sixteen years old. Am I right?" He nodded sheepishly.

Then I asked, "How old do you feel like?" No answer. "I'll guess, and you tell me if I'm right. Seven?" He gave an uncertain yes/no response.

Upon further inquiry, I learned that he was not the youngest in the family, having a sister aged thirteen.

"Oh dear," I said. "You were only three years old when she was born. I bet your mother was so busy with the new baby that you felt left out." He nodded in agreement. "You must have felt real bad." Again he indicated agreement. "How did your older brothers treat you?" I asked.

"They was good to me. They don't like my sister either."

I asked, "You still feel mad at your sister?"

"Yeah, I hate her. She cusses and everything."

"Oh, poor sister," I said. "She's probably spoiled and feels bad that her brothers don't like her." He agreed.

"Tell me about your brothers. Would you like to be like them?"

"Naw, not the eighteen-year-old. He dropped out of school. But I like the twenty-year-old," he replied.

"Is he smart and grown-up acting?"

"Yeah."

Then I said, *"I have an idea. Can you imagine that you have your older brother's feelings inside you? Like, in your heart you feel and act just like him?"*

His eyes looked thoughtful as he nodded.

"O.K. I wonder how many times today you will be able to see that scene in your mind."

"Lots."

"Can you see it all day today and tomorrow and then on Saturday and Sunday?"

"Yes," he replied.

"Only one thing," I cautioned. "Don't tell anyone. It's got to be a secret, OK?"

"OK." We smiled conspiratorially and said goodbye for now.

Seventh Period: Mitchel enters the classroom and sits in a different seat from his usual one. He behaves in a model manner the whole period, even when some of the others are being less than attentive.

At the beginning of the period, I go over to him and ask if he remembered to see the scene. He replies, "I was seeing it all day." I then remind him again that it is to be kept secret. He smiles.

His mature behavior lasted about a week. Then he came into class on a Monday and sat in his old seat, behaving more like he used to. When I questioned him about it, he said, *"You said I should be like that for a week."* (!!)

Note: The next time I encounter such a situation, I'll make a Milton Ericson type of indirect suggestion, such as, *"I wonder how it will feel when June comes, and you get a report card with all A's and with comments about how grown-up you are."*

Corinna Puts Me Down

Upon entering the special ed office, I found Corinna, Tom, and Jose sitting around the table. I sat down and began to chat, asking what they were doing there. Corinna, obviously feeling an implied reprimand, asked me why I was so hard to get along with, indicating that many people felt that way about me. Three years ago, Corinna was in my class, and since then our only encounters have been my finding her in the special ed office as though she were one of the staff, or hanging out in the corridor during class hours.

I responded that many other people do not find me hard to get along with. If she knew of some who do, it wouldn't matter to me, since my interest was not to be popular, but to try to help students learn to think well enough to take care of themselves, especially after they were through with school.

She politely accused me further of butting into her business when she was doing something that didn't concern me. Her argument was that if she chose to cut a class and take a chance of getting into trouble, it was not my affair to question her.

I replied that it's the responsibility of every teacher to call a student to task who is breaking a rule, whether the student happens to be in one of her classes or not. I then invited her to imagine how she would act if she were a teacher in a circumstance similar to mine.

She immediately said that she didn't know how she would act, but I said I understood that, and I wasn't asking her what she *thought* she would do. I wanted her to run a movie in her mind and see herself as "Miss Smith, a teacher in the school." I asked her to witness the scene, as though she were the audience watching the action. We had to part at that moment, but she said she would do the imaging and let me know what she saw.

About ten minutes later we met again, and she told me she saw that she would intercede the way I had done. I felt validated and, surprisingly, more tolerant of her. We parted with what felt like a greater sense of mutual respect.

Cutting Math Class—A Band-Aid Remedy

Kenny complained that he doesn't like to go to his math class, because he doesn't know the teacher or the kids. Therefore, he "freezes" when he is in such an environment. When he has to take a test, he can't even answer the questions he knows.

My Plan: Use *Eidetic Imagery* for overcoming the problem.

Procedure:

1. I asked Kenny where he feels the freezing when he's in math class. He said he feels it in his head; not the rest of his body.

2. I asked him to see himself entering the math room.

MG: *What do you see?*

Kenny: *I'm walking into the room. I see the kids, the desks, etc.*

MG: *What is the expression on your face?*

Kenny: *Angry.*

MG: *What's happening now?*

Kenny: *I'm sitting down with my paper and beginning to freeze.*

3. I then had him take a break (still in imagery) like an actor. He was to breathe in the warm, relaxing sunshine.

4. We repeated the same scene, as in 2 above, but more slowly. He reported two changes as follows:

   a) He no longer looked angry.

   b) Upon taking the test, he first froze, then unfroze briefly, then refroze.

5. We took a second break. He inhaled the sunshine again.

6. We repeated the scene a third time, in slow motion. This time he reported taking the whole test, with no freezing.

He agreed to re-visualize the math scene many times during his detention that day, and also before going to bed that night. He agreed also to do the visualization every day.

After the imagery, he began doing his English assignment and worked diligently for the remainder of the period, without his usual interruptions for socializing. The next day he did not cut his math class, as he had been in the habit of doing, and the math teacher reported unusually cooperative behavior.

Note: Why do I call this a "band-aid?" Because I did not have the time to follow through with the necessary individual attention on successive days. He needed follow-up supplemental exercises in order to sustain the new behavior and have it become habitual.

A Hyperactive Student—An Experiment

Luis, a ninth-grader, was extremely hyperactive. He meant well but couldn't sit still or keep his attention on the lesson. Since this behavior interfered with the progress of the whole class, I suggested an experiment as follows:

For three days, eat no sweets (candy, pastry, soda pop, gum). At first Luis objected, "What! I eat candy every day!" He put his head down on his desk in a gesture of despair. Then he agreed to try it.

I advised him to imagine himself looking at candy, etc., and smiling calmly as he waved them away with his hand.

Immediately, Philip announced that Luis would be unable

to succeed in this project and began reciting names of candy in a tempting tone. Gradually most of the other boys joined in trying to discourage him. One boy said Luis would get killed by a truck. Another merely predicted that he would fail. I was amazed at the anger the suggestion generated.

Luis responded by covering his ears with his hands. I advised him to listen instead, and to use the opportunity to practice resisting temptation. The following were my suggestions:

1) As the words came at him he was to smile and inwardly wave them away.

2) As the attempts became louder and more aggressive, he was to continue smiling, and say aloud, "You're right," retaining his inward hand-waving.

The next day, when I encountered Luis in the corridor, he said that he did feel calmer today and was able to sit quietly during his first-period class. For supper last night he had rice and beans, salad, and milk. Breakfast consisted of egg, bacon, and milk. Lunch was tuna sandwich, salad, and milk.

He told me that Philip gave him a candy that morning, and he (Luis) "shot it on the floor."

He looked pleased, and I complimented him upon his calm response to the challenges in class yesterday.

In my class he behaved very well. When Gregg tried to tease him, Luis simply agreed with him. Philip punched him in the chest in frustration, but Luis remained calmly seated.

P.S. Ultimately, Philip and the others "won". As was to be expected, Luis was unable to stay with this non-sugar diet. Like most of us, Luis couldn't "kick the habit" without some strong home support and the ability to find satisfying sub-

stitutes for his sugar craving. Unhappily, he had neither.

It's possible, however, that not all is lost. Perhaps in the future he will remember this way of remaining calm, if others try to upset or tease him.

Miracle in Room 154

It happened during my largest reading class (fourteen students). During oral drill on the short sound of *O*, Anita (a student new to my class) suddenly complained, "This is stupid! I'm not going to do this stupid stuff. I'm getting changed out of this class."

I informed her that if she intended to change classes, she should tell her counselor, not me and the whole class.

She replied that she's not the only one who feels that way. *"They all think it's stupid."*

To my amazement, one of the boys immediately turned to her and said, *"Who's 'they'? I don't think it's stupid."*

Jonathan echoed this statement, while several others disagreed with Anita in one way or another.

Not another word of complaint from Anita since then. After eleven years of teaching, who would ever expect such a dream-come-true? It felt like a miracle!

Stan's Outrage

Stan was abnormally sensitive to corrections or even suggestions and found put-downs where none were intended. He often entered my class complaining angrily about a previous teacher, and once he started, it was hard to get him to stop talking. In fact, if allowed, he could use up the entire class time, with each complaint generating another one.

Such an event threatened to take place this morning. Stan was outraged and fuming about the teacher of his previous class. When I questioned whether he understood the teacher's message, he became even more incensed, defending himself by saying that he has pride, and no one can push him around. *"These big-shot teachers think they can do anything they want,"* etc.

Finally, I made a split-second decision and began to act as though I were just as furious as he. I got on my high horse and began to complain loudly that *he couldn't talk to me like that—I had feelings, too—just because he was bigger than me—just because I was only a teacher*, etc. After a couple of minutes I stopped, apologized briefly to the rest of the class, and then began the reading lesson.

To my surprise, Stan quietly participated in the oral reading with a chastened and cooperative demeanor, and made no further complaints.

After the period was over, the previous teacher—at whom he was so angry—called him into his room and explained what he had tried to communicate in the first place. This time Stan was able to hear him, and they parted amicably.

For the remainder of the year, Stan behaved in a more mature and friendly manner, even when he was feeling out of sorts. At such times, he would come into the room and explain that he was feeling bad and would apologize for not being up to participating in the lesson.

Note: It's clear that Stan had never thought that teachers, as well as students, could feel vulnerable. He resented the fact that teachers seemed to have all the power and were not held accountable to act in a fair and respectful manner toward students. While there may be some validity to this grievance, I believe that my histrionics opened his eyes to the fact that teachers were human beings who had feelings, just as he had.

Monte Does Some Growing

Mr. M told me he was having trouble with his fourth-period math class because of the constant disruptions by Monte and Billy. I offered to speak with Monte, and the following is a brief account of our talk:

First, I reminded him that he once had said he didn't want me to have such high expectations of him. He remembered, but said he didn't feel that way any more. I told him I was glad to hear that. I also told him that over the years there were a few students that stood out in my memory more than the rest, and whom I remembered with happy feelings. I told him I believed he was one of the students whom I would always remember.

I then broached the subject at hand by saying that different teachers and students affect each other differently. When teachers are having a hard time with a particular student or class, they will often talk to another teacher—not for the sake of gossip, but because they're looking for help. They might say, *"I'm having a problem dealing with this kid; you seem to have a good relationship with him. Any suggestions?"*

Monte indicated he understood and wasn't offended when I told him I was seeing him because Mr. M was unhappy with his behavior. He readily acknowledged that he and Billy were a difficult pair.

Then I explained that when Mr. M scolds them for acting disrespectfully and likens them to drug dealers, it's not because he thinks they *are* drug dealers. He's talking like that because he wants them to grow up to be respectable. He doesn't want them to shame their parents or their race. Mr. M is African-American, as are Monte and Billy, and he identifies with them, *like a father would.* (I know Monte misses his father, who died when Monte was a little boy.)

I pointed out that I learned a lot from *my* father, but he made mistakes just like any human being, and just like Mr. M does sometimes. We must forgive mistakes, and know that our father—or teacher—is trying to help us.

"Can't you imagine how angry your father would be if you fooled around in class? He could accuse you of acting like a drug dealer, not because he believes you are one, but because he's angry. He wants you to be more respectful. He wants you to grow up to be a good man: proud, honest, and respectable."

Monte looked serious. I continued. *"Can you imagine yourself in math class, ignoring Billy when he acts up? Maybe Billy will be angry with you, but sometimes when we care about people, we have to do things that will make them angry. Can you imagine that scene, where you're ignoring Billy and being respectful to Mr. M—who is being **like your father?"***

I was silent, allowing Monte to experience the scene inwardly. Then he said, *"I got it."*

I thanked him for coming to talk, and he went back to Mr. M's class. Later in the day, Mr. M phoned to thank me, saying that Monte had behaved perfectly the whole period, doing his work quietly and paying complete attention. *"Even if it doesn't last, it was worth it for today, and I appreciate it."*

Note: Monte's good behavior could be reinforced for the future by having him mentally preview his behavior before each class.

Chapter Eight

Disrespectful Class

S.O.S:
When I feel frustrated or Angry with a Disrespectful or Unappreciative Class (or Student)

What Do I Do?

I abruptly stop teaching to sit down and write notes to the student(s) or to myself about the disturbing experience. It often helps to raise my awareness of how to deal with the situation, and, at the very least, it gives me something to do with my anger.

Chaos in the Classroom

I am trying to get the students to apply the strategies of problem-solving to the purchase of a new car. There are eleven people in the class, three or four of whom look interested and behave respectfully. The others, however, are uncooperative.

One person, for example, is worried that people are talking about him, so he defensively complains to me. One girl is angry because I had given her a detention earlier. One boy frequently interrupts with questions and comments that have nothing to do with the subject; sometimes he understands this; sometimes he doesn't. Two girls keep whispering at the back of the room. One boy deliberately interrupts with foolish comments and knows they are foolish.

I become aware that I am talking louder and louder, trying to get them to listen. Finally, I decide it's not possible to continue trying to teach the lesson. Without another word, I sit down, ignoring the students, and turn to writing an account of the current situation. I realize that inevitably there are times when the wisest course is to distance myself from things. The students want to know what I'm writing, so I read this account aloud and then ask them to imagine themselves as the teacher. They are to watch this mental movie and discover the best way to handle the situation.

The bell rings as I am talking.

Countering the Distracting Vibes

During another class, the students were distracted and inattentive, and I felt it would have been an uphill battle to try teaching in such an atmosphere. I decided that one way to get them to settle down and listen would be to tell them I was going to give a character reading of how I saw each student. They immediately became attentive.

First, I said I had noticed a general change in student behavior over the past two years. While they *looked* much like previous students, on the whole they were less mature. I thought they were intelligent and nice, and quite grown-up looking. But *inside*, their feelings were more like little children.

There was one young man in particular whom I considered to be very good-looking, tall, and intelligent, but his emotional development in some ways was about five years old. Roger asked who that was, and I told him it was himself. To my relief, he didn't seem to take offense. He was surprised, however, at the age I had said. "Five?" he asked, as though meaning "not nine or ten?"

I reminded him of his earlier habit of saying things like "I'm not coming to school any more" when he was offended by a teacher's reprimand. Then I acknowledged that recently he was handling his feelings better than he used to.

Corman asked what I thought of **his** emotional age, and I guessed "about nine." I added that he could be quite stubborn, and he agreed "at times." I further told him that he had the mistaken idea that teachers were trying to trap him when they asked him questions, when all they wanted to know was whether they had explained a rule or an idea clearly. He acknowledged that he "used to" be like that.

Ana at first said she didn't want me to "read" her, but immediately changed her mind. I remarked that last year I was delighted to have her as a student because she learned so readily. She acknowledged, by nodding in agreement, that she had learned much about reading. I added that I was disappointed when she spoke to me disrespectfully, as if I didn't have feelings because I was a teacher. She listened seriously.

Berna listened attentively, nodding when I said her reading had improved very much last year. When I added that emotionally she had grown up a lot, she smiled in agreement, and I felt rewarded by her expression.

Terrie had come a long way also. Last year she'd had a little bit of devil in her and cut class a lot. But this year she seemed more grown-up, and even though she could get quite angry with some kids, on the whole she was acting calmer and more mature. She smiled in appreciation.

Gino kept his head down as I described his previous year, when he'd been in my class with only two other kids. Sometimes he'd say he wasn't going to participate, but most of the time we would have a good lesson. I didn't know why he never took part this year. I wasn't able to give him the same attention as I had the previous year because his reading class was so much larger now. I got the feeling that he appreciated what I was saying, and that he felt a bit sad and even puzzled about his behavior during the current year.

I turned to Irene and observed that she must feel bad a lot, because she asks to go to the nurse or her counselor so often. She agreed with this assessment.

On the whole, I believe the students felt validated, and we then proceeded to have a good lesson.

The Compliments Game

The students were being disagreeable to each other, so I announced that we would each say something nice about every person. The individual whose turn it was would also comment. I spoke first each time. We began by giving Gladys our attention, as follows:

Gladys

- Mrs. G: *Gladys is generous and kind. She could learn better if she were more relaxed. She cares about other people and is very supportive.*

- Gladys: *I know how to wait when the teacher is busy. I like to read. I like the teachers.*

- Nardo: *She is nice, understands. Sometimes she is out of control, but calms down and apologizes. Honest lady. Good attendance. Prompt.*

- Marie: *Nice person. Helps me when I need it. Fun to be with.*

- Mariela: *Good student. I help her. She helps people. Teaches herself.*

Nardo

- Mrs. G: *Fair, kind, brave, polite, helpful, friendly, smart. Cares about himself and other people. Nice smile.*

- Nardo: *I am a comedian.* [He means he sometimes "cuts up" in class.] *Sometimes I'm not responsible. I forget my pen, book; sometimes late to class. Sometimes have a bad attitude; short temper.*

- Gladys: *Nice person. Nice to me. Helps me with work.*

- Marie: *Helpful, friendly, nice person.*

- Mariela: *Nice person. Good student. Helps people. Responsible.*

Marie

- Mrs. G: *Speaks nicely. Nice voice. Polite. Doesn't inter-*

rupt. Acts like a lady.

- Marie: *I'm a good worker. Not lazy.*
- Nardo: *Smart. Good attendance. Good student.*
- Gladys: *Helps me with my work. I am grateful. I help her because she is my friend. She asks to use my books nice.*
- Mariela: *Quiet. Reads. Talks sometimes.*

Robert

- Mrs. G: *A little shy. Good student. Learns well. Friendly.*
- Marie: *Nice person. Nice looking. Nice smile.*
- Nardo: *Nice guy. I'd like to be his friend. Responsible member of the class. Does his work all the time.*
- Gladys: *Nice person. If he needs help, he asks me.*
- Mariela: *Nice boy. Quiet. A pleasure to have in class.*

Mariela

- Mrs.G: *Often tries hard. Kind. Cares about herself and others. Can relax. Lovely smile. Friendly.*
- Mariela: *Responsible. I keep my word.*
- Nardo: *Good sense of humor. Responsible to work. Keeps her promise. Not rude. Respectful most of the time to teacher. Friendly.*
- Gladys: *Nice girl. Talks nice to me. Sometimes I buy her something. When I need help, she helps me.*
- Marie: *Nice person. Does her work. Behaves in class.*

Mrs. Gifford

- Mrs.G: *I try my best to teach and learn. I care about students, myself, and others.*

- Nardo: *Nice teacher. If students got a problem, they can talk to her and she can solve the problem. Helps them improve their language. On time to class.*

- Gladys: *She always help, when you need something, like to eat or help.*

- Marie: *Nice person. Helps us when we need it.*

- Mariela: *Nice teacher. Takes a joke. Sometimes gets mad for me and Gladys laughing too much.*

After the exercise, it was evident that the students were feeling happier about themselves and with each other. They hear so many negative comments about themselves, and basically feel so bad about being "special ed" and having reading problems, that it's important to find opportunities that will, at least temporarily, raise their spirits and self-image.

Chapter Nine

Unacceptable Behaviors

Defusing a Fight through Imagery Mediation

David came into the class, minus his usual warm greeting. Instead of sitting at the table with us as he usually does in this small class, he went to the opposite side of the room, saying that he was not going to participate in the lesson because he didn't want to get into a fight.

I soon learned that David and Naldo had had a fight in their previous class. Before I could say a word, Naldo was shouting at David and threatening to get him after school. David responded by getting out of his seat and approaching Naldo menacingly. I managed to get David to sit back down and asked him not to say anything else, no matter what Naldo might say. He sat down with his back toward us but didn't agree to remain silent.

I went to the table where Naldo was sitting with the other students and asked if he would tell me quietly what had happened. I said that David would not interrupt and would have his turn later. I told Naldo that to make sure I understood him, I would write down the things he said and repeat back what I heard. He agreed. Here is an outline of his report:

● *"Him"* (pointing at David) *"and Herman were joking in Ms. X's room. Herman said to David, 'You look like a cracker.' I thought Herman said that because David had yellow on his jacket, and cheese crackers are yellow."*

● *"I wanted to joke with them too, so I said to David, 'You look like a cheese cracker.'"*

● *"David got mad and got up and said, 'Do you want to do something about it?'"*

● *"I was first a little bit surprised, and then I felt insulted and angry."* (These last adjectives were offered by me, and Naldo said they fit his feelings at the time.) *"I felt to myself, 'He's not going to push me around.'"*

● *"I got up, and the teacher was holding me and then let go, because she thought it was safe."*

● *"I picked up a chair and threw it at David."*

● *"David threw it back, and I caught it."*

● *"The teacher took me out of the room to Mr. M's room till the period was over."*

I repeated the account to check that I understood (while David listened with his back toward us). Then I asked Naldo to repeat the scene again, seeing everything in his mind as he talked. After he finished, I asked if he knew anybody—boy or man—who is very calm and grown-up. He said, "Yes, my Uncle Tony."

"OK," I replied. "Now I want you to go through the scene again, but this time you are to step into Tony's shoes and feel Tony inside you."

"You want me to be Tony?"

"Yes."

He closed his eyes and reported the scene as he watched it again. After reporting that David got angry and challenged him, Naldo (with Tony's mature attitude) said, *"Oh, hey Bo, I'm sorry. I thought you were only joking. I didn't mean anything."*

After the scene was over, I asked Naldo if he still felt angry. He responded, *"I don't know. I'm not angry at David. I wish David wouldn't be angry."*

David was now facing the rest of us and looked calm and relaxed. The tension and danger had left the room and the atmosphere was suddenly friendly.

I asked the boys if they would like to visit each other at their homes sometimes. They replied that it wouldn't be possible because they lived in different neighborhoods, and it would be dangerous to be seen in the wrong neighborhood. David lived on Park Street, while Naldo lived at the "The Square." If one wandered into the other's territory, he would get jumped by gang members. I asked if they could at least walk to classes together. Again they informed me that such behavior would be dangerous. They would get jumped, even in school.

From there the conversation moved to a discussion of gangs in general, with my asking questions and their being the authorities. Both boys belong to their neighborhood gangs. David said there are gangs everywhere, all over the country, in every city. When I asked why they belong to a gang, the response was that it was for protection, "like a family."

The situation seems to be growing worse all the time. Every day the vice-principals are busy with the police, while their offices are overflowing with insubordinate students sent out of the room by their teachers.

It seems to be the ninth-graders, mostly, who are in trouble. Every teacher with whom I've spoken agrees that this new crop of freshmen is "extraordinarily immature." The teachers in suburban areas, as well, are finding that their current ninth-graders act as though they don't understand how one is supposed to behave in school—talking out at will, complaining about the teaching, and outraged at expectations of decorum.

When people wonder what has caused this sudden worsening of student behaviors, I think of multiple factors, not the least of which are the broken families and the continual violence, both on television and in their neighborhoods. While most of us feel less safe than we did even ten years ago, I believe that the children feel much, much worse, especially those in the inner cities.

A Note to Tom and Sam

To: Tom and Sam
From: Mrs. Gifford

As you probably realize, I am quite proud of both of you boys. You have made wonderful progress since I first knew you. Progress in thinking, listening, talking, and reading—and also progress in responsible behavior.

But I have a little problem. It appears that you have important things to discuss with each other. I think students need more time for this, but we have only 42 minutes for our lesson. I find it very hard to teach when 2 of my star pupils are ignoring me.

I don't know what to do about it. Can you solve this problem?

Thanks.

MOG

Note: Their behavior changed for the better after this, although they never mentioned the note to me.

The Story of Carlton — Bully Behavior

It was between periods, and we were standing in the hall outside our classrooms. The social studies teacher told me that Carlton had just kicked Elwood in the stomach, and that he, the teacher, then sent Elwood straight to the vice-principal to report the assault.

Since the next period was my planning time, I asked the teacher to permit Carlton to spend the time with me. He consented.

I asked Carlton to tell me what had happened, and he said that he and Elwood were just kidding around; "no big deal." In the hope of getting him to tell the episode more truthfully, I asked Carlton if he would try some imagery exercises. He consented, although a bit warily.

I told him to close his eyes and remember the episode as though he were watching a movie. He was to tell me what was happening as he watched. He reported the action in a rapid fashion, in the past tense. It was obvious that he was not viewing a movie in his mind, but was trying to get it over with, telling me as little detail as possible.

I had him relax a moment, and then I instructed him to repeat the action, in slow motion. His version went like this: *"Elwood's walking down the hall toward me, and I'm standing against the lockers. Then I go up to him and put my hands on his chest, fooling around like tickling him."*

I asked Carlton to look at Elwood in the image, and tell me how Elwood was feeling. Carlton replied that Elwood was laughing. Since Carlton made no mention of kicking Elwood, I asked him about it. He replied that he was just kidding around, and had kicked him lightly in the stomach. With further prompting, he reported that Elwood walked away and said, *"Faggot."*

After the third telling, I asked Carlton to imagine himself walking down the hall. He was to see a big rough fellow walk up to him, put his hands on his chest and then kick him in the stomach. *"How do you feel when that happens?"* I asked.

He replied, *"Kinda scared, I guess."*

I advised him that when the vice principal called him to her office, he would be wise not to lie or pretend innocence. At that moment, the vice-principal phoned my room, requesting that Carlton come to see her. Before he left, I suggested that his Guardian Angel could fill him with white light and surround him like a halo. He could keep this light around him as he walked to the office. He thanked me and left.

A short time later, I saw Elwood in the corridor and asked what happened at the office. He said that Carlton had walked in quietly and apologized. He told the vice-principal that he had been doing imagery with me. Then, according to Elwood, the vice-principal commended Carlton for walking in like a gentleman and behaving as he had.

Elwood was not impressed. In fact, he still doubted that Carlton could be trusted. When I asked Elwood to tell me about the episode in the hall, he reported that he felt angry when Carlton rubbed his hands over his chest. When Elwood protested, Carlton kicked him in the stomach. Then Carlton grabbed him by the shirt and said *"That'll teach you to respect me."* Elwood added that Carlton accused him of saying some word (which Elwood couldn't remember). I supplied the word, *"Faggot?"* and he said that was the word, and that he hadn't said it. I felt quite angry at hearing this addition to the story, and wondered if there was anything I could say to Carlton that would make an impression.

The next morning he said "hello" to me in a warm and loving way as he passed me in the hall. I was standing outside my room, talking to a teacher, and he put his hand on my shoulder in a gentle manner as he passed behind me. It felt like a gesture of gratitude, and I wondered if his attitude toward Elwood and his own behavior, as well, had changed.

Each day for the next few days, I asked Elwood about Carlton's behavior toward him. At first, Elwood reported that Carlton had not said or done anything nasty, but indicated that he still didn't trust him. After a couple of weeks, however, when Carlton was still treating him respectfully, Elwood acknowledged that his hard feelings toward Carlton had dissipated, and that Carlton was OK.

By this time it was the last week of school before summer vacation. I was visiting with a colleague in my room during lunch period, when Carlton appeared at my door. He said he was planning not to return to school in the fall and wanted to wish me well. As he hugged me and said goodbye, I was touched by the sense of gratitude that I felt from him.

Chapter Ten

The Aikido Attitude

In the Aikido philosophy, one wins by using the energy of one's opponent. Instead of resisting or fighting back, the Aikido practitioner moves aside or away. Thus, for example, instead of trying to block a blow, he moves out of the way and allows the opponent to fall from his own momentum. Similarly, in verbal disagreements, an Aikido person would not argue. Instead, she would allow the opponent room to change his mind, since she would not struggle against him. The following episodes illustrate how such an orientation can help defuse situations which threaten to become confrontative or painful, and which no one "wins".

Sylvia Role-Plays: A Defense Against Teasing

Sylvia is a friendly girl who enjoys bantering with the boys. During the second week of school, I was testing individual students and allowed the others to talk quietly. I noticed that the boys were teasing Sylvia with put-down remarks.

She would answer them by saying, "I don't think so," evidently finding this to be a sophisticated way to handle the repartee.

I spoke to her privately about the boys' disrespectful way of teasing, but she said, "They're only playing." The following day the teasing worsened, and she became insulted. She responded to them in kind (by saying something in Spanish) and they all laughed, much to her anger.

When the bell rang at the end of the class period, I asked her to stay behind for a moment. I asked if she would role-play the episode, with me being Sylvia, and her being the boy who had insulted her. She consented.

First we played the incident as it happened:

> Boy: *"You're a bandijo."*
> Sylvia: *"**You're** a bandijo."* (That's when they all laughed.)

Then we played the incident from an *Aikido* perspective:

> Boy: *"You're a bandijo."*
> Sylvia: *"I feel very bad when you say that to me."*

Sylvia, playing the part of the boy, looked surprised at my second response. I asked her how she felt when I (as Sylvia) answered the second time. She said she felt bad, and made it clear that the role-play was helpful to her. She thanked me as she got up and left for her next class.

Note: *At various times, this type of Aikido application has been helpful to other children. A third-grader whom I taught in summer school didn't want to go out to recess because the boys called her "fat," and she would cry and go back to the classroom early.*

I suggested that she answer them by saying, "I feel bad

when you call me fat."

She agreed to try it that same day, and after recess she happily reported that they apologized and stopped their insults.

Gilberto Insists upon Conventional Lessons

Occasionally, teachers encounter students who are so turned off or discouraged that they apparently have lost all hope of learning anything meaningful. They may reject challenges or anything different. They wish merely to continue with the activities they have become accustomed to over the years, despite the fact that these have failed them.

When such a student encounters my unusual way of teaching and complains to me about it, I find that it's best not to argue or pull rank. If I can find a way to honor the student's views (true to my Aikido philosophy), the student will often come around. The story of Gilberto is an example of such a change in attitude.

Gilberto was in my "Intensive Reading Class" and couldn't read, even on a first-grade level. His behavior alternated between hyperactivity and keeping his head down on his desk. He expressed great impatience with the oral part of the lessons, saying, *"We did this already."* He would have liked a "new thing" every day. I told him that if I were to teach the way he'd been used to, he would continue to learn nothing. I said he **needed** to have drill with the "same thing" many, many times, if he was to remember the material.

He confused pronouns, vocabulary, directional words, and grammar. On the rare occasions when he cooperated, he showed ability to learn and to change. Furthermore, he acknowledged that he **did** understand that the oral lessons were necessary, agreeing that he must learn to talk in an understandable way.

Instead of my unconventional program, however, he still preferred a more typical class, in which students spent the time writing quietly in their workbooks.

I explained that such a method hadn't worked for him all these years, but if that was what he wanted, that's what I'd permit him to do. I told him to think about it and to make the choice. At the end of the class period, I asked if he'd decided whether he wanted me to teach him tomorrow.

Yeah.

My *way of teaching?*

Yeah.

I actually didn't have much hope that he would stick seriously to the lessons. He was absent the next day, because of a doctor's appointment. However, the following Monday Gilberto behaved cooperatively the entire period, with no complaints whatsoever.

Several weeks later, before the class began, Gilberto was working on a math project titled, "Parts of an inch." He had drawn a reproduction of a ruler, but was using the millimeter edge instead of the inches for measurements. When I tried to correct him, he became angry and said that that was the way his friend had done it. He refused to listen to me. I sensed that he was replaying the tone of voice that he and his mother would use toward each other when they were angry.

Therefore, instead of arguing, I talked to him about feeling defensive when someone says you are wrong. I role-played his mother's yelling at him, imitating the angry tone he had used with me. (*You're so lazy! Your room is a mess!* and so on.) I also played the part of Gilberto himself, yelling back at his mother. He indicated that in general, it matched his experiences. I then demonstrated an Aikido-type of reply that he could use in such a situation:

Close your eyes, and in your mind look at your mother's face after you yell at her. How does she look? Mad? Not mad? Feels sorry?

Gilberto kept his eyes closed, but refused to talk. I watched him as his breathing deepened. Then I replayed the scene, but this time I changed Gilberto's response, as follows:

See your mother yelling at you. (pause)

See yourself saying, "I'm sorry for what I did. I can see that you're very mad at me." (Validating his mother's feelings. Again I paused.)

Look at your mother's face now. (Gilberto took a deep breath.)

How does she look? Mad? Not mad? Feels sorry?

Gilberto replied, *"She feels sorry."*

What does she do now?

Gilberto didn't answer; but Anthony, who had been watching the scene in his own mind, said, *"She walks away."* I watched Gilberto; he took a deep breath, looking much relieved.

In the above situation, I chose an Aikido type of response instead of arguing with his childish stubbornness. I addressed his emotional state, hoping at least to alleviate some of his anger. He appeared to appreciate it. Thus, although he didn't learn much about using a ruler, at least he had an experi-

ence that had some emotional benefit.

Incident with Tina – A Type of Aikido?

*This story is reminiscent of the one about Randy in Chapter Seven. In each case, a person was treating me with disrespect. In each case when I spoke up and identified their intention, they immediately dropped their unfriendly behavior. Yet the two situations were quite different. In Randy's case, I avoided the need to punish **him**; in Tina's case, I avoided possible punishment for **myself** by not responding defensively to my accuser. In each instance, my Aikido-style response turned an unpleasant situation into a positive one.*

It was the day before winter vacation. On my desk were some valentines addressed to students. A few girls began picking up the valentines, peeking inside to see who had written them. I was shocked and ordered the girls to put them down. Everyone complied except Tina, who continued to pry. In my frustration, I suddenly heard myself telling Tina that she was a nosy ___ . I believe I was more surprised at what I said than Tina was.

Tina huffed out of the room, saying no one could talk to her like that. I immediately called her vice-principal and related the incident. He said she was in his office, telling him about the matter, and wanted him to do something about it. This was the last day of school before vacation week.

Upon returning from vacation, I was informed that there was to be a meeting in the principal's office about the matter. Present at the meeting were the principal, two vice-principals (Magnet Program vice-principal and regular vice-principal), Tina, her aunt (Ms. M), and myself.

At the outset of the meeting, Ms. M said that she expected a written apology from me for what I had said to Tina, but that an apology, in itself, would not be the end of the matter. She made it clear that if I weren't properly dealt with by the principal (i.e., getting suspended for three days,) she would take the complaint to the Board of Education.

Mr. C, the principal, responded calmly and forthrightly, with courtesy and fairness, and all present had their say. I thought they all spoke very well, including Ms. M.

Ms. M repeated that she expected an apology and more, and said that Tina had written one to me last night for her part in the episode. Tina then produced a folded note from her pocket. I was somewhat touched and said I didn't need a note; if Tina was sincere, that was all that mattered to me.

After an hour and a quarter of talking, mostly by Mr. C and Ms. M, I made the observation to Ms. M that it sounded as though she wasn't so much interested in helping me to become a better teacher as she was in getting revenge. A moment later, to my great surprise, Ms. M said she respected me for not claiming that Tina had misunderstood what I had said. Suddenly her attitude completely changed. She was no longer out for blood!

The atmosphere in the room transformed into one of warmth and respect. I asked Tina what she needed from me, because I didn't want her to feel mistreated. If she felt a written apology was important, I could oblige. She seemed a bit confused, but indicated she didn't need one. All talk of retribution vanished.

Mr. C asked a question of Tina: *"What would you have preferred to have happened as a consequence of your behav-*

ior?" Seemingly taken aback, Tina answered that she would have preferred a three-day suspension. At that, I expressed surprise, saying I'd take being called a name much sooner than getting suspended.

The meeting had lasted an hour-and-a-half, but it was worth it, ending with handshakes and warm feelings all around. I felt that, much to my amazement, I had found a friend in the aunt. The aunt certainly couldn't have felt she was given short shrift, so perhaps something was learned in terms of human relations and communication. After this dramatic episode, Tina's behavior in my homeroom changed greatly for the better. Whenever I needed a student to help me or to run an errand, Tina was always the first to volunteer eagerly, with courtesy and a smile!!

Chapter Eleven

When Students
Are Upset

Gino Finds His Wisdom

When a student enters my classroom in a rage, I try to help him deal with the anger before expecting him to pay attention to the lesson. In this episode, I present a young man who habitually responded to authority in an insulted and sulky manner. I helped him find a way to preserve his feelings and behave more appropriately. Here is the story:

There was only one other student in the classroom when Gino entered, looking very angry. I tried to ask about his problem, but he growled, *"Never mind. Just sign this,"* as he pushed a paper toward me. The paper was to inform teachers that he was returning from suspension. I left the paper where it was and decided to address his attitude instead, especially since a reading lesson under these circumstances would probably have proved fruitless.

I asked why he had been suspended and learned that he'd had an incident with the science teacher. He told me he had been holding a card, and that she said, "Put your card away." He argued that he was wearing sweats with no pockets, and that his book bag was across the room. If he got up to get it, he said, he'd receive a detention for walking around. She warned him again to put it away. When he continued to argue, she said *"We'll talk about it after school,"* to which he responded, *"I ain't gonna stay for no detention. I never stay for nobody."* The vice-principal suspended him.

I acknowledged how angry he was, and said I understood how hard it is to act respectfully to the teacher in the next class when you're feeling so angry. He nodded in agreement. Then we talked about how we learn to control feelings as we grow older. When babies are angry, they're angry all over —arms-legs-face—crying loudly. It doesn't matter who approaches them; they act angry to everyone.

But in high school, if you feel angry, you don't want to be mean toward someone you're not mad at. Yet you don't want to ignore your bad feelings and pretend you're happy. What can you do? He didn't know, so I said we'd role-play it: he was to be me, and I'd be Gino.

We role-played the conversation we'd had when he first entered my class. When he (as teacher) asked why I was angry, I turned to him and said irritably, *"Never mind. Just sign this."*

Then we repeated the scene. This time I (as Gino) turned to "the teacher" and said, *"I feel so mad; that teacher just yelled at me. I'm not mad at you, but I still feel very angry."*

Gino indicated that as the teacher, he felt better in the second scene. He looked more relaxed.

Then I tackled the earlier incident with the science teacher. He was unwilling at first to role-play, saying *"Just tell me what I should say."* I replied that my words wouldn't really help him. He had to learn from inside himself. I reminded him of the times when I would be teaching him to read and to spell words by writing the letters in his mind until he could see the whole word. Then he would know it, learning it from within his own mind.

We proceeded with the role-play: I was Gino and he was Ms. R, the science teacher. The first scene was re-enacted as it happened. In the replay, after he (as Ms. R) told me (Gino) to put away the card, I whispered, *"I don't know what to do; I'll ask my Guardian Angel."* I turned to Gino and whispered, *"What should I do?"* He replied, *"Put it under your paper, and she won't see it, so you'll be all right."* I did as he recommended, and he was all smiles.

After that, I began the reading part of the lesson, with two cheerful and cooperative students.

Note: This role-playing strategy enabled Gino to rise above his helpless, "mistreated" self-image for once. In its place he was able to get in touch with his own wisdom and discovered for himself an answer that was both mature and effective.

Johnny Deals with His Angry Feelings

Johnny told me that he was brought to the vice-principal because he refused to participate in gym. He said that the teacher gets angry because they play games and Johnny doesn't want to play.

MG: *But games are fun, aren't they?*

J: *Yes, but if I'm mad, how am I going to play?*

MG: *I see. You have to feel good to play. If you play, what are you going to do with your mad feelings, is that it?*

J: *Right. I have to go off by myself when I'm mad.*

I commented that teachers and bosses usually aren't concerned with whether or not a person is mad. They just have to be obeyed or else. And they're the ones with the power to fire you or to get you into trouble. He agreed.

MG: *I have an idea. When you enter the gym, if you feel mad, you can sweep the mad feelings into a corner of your mind and close the door. But tell the feelings that you promise to pay attention to them later—after school. Be sweet and polite to the feelings. Then you can be free to participate in the game. Want to try it?*

J: *OK.*

Leading him step by step, I instructed him to see the gym class episode in his mind.

MG: *See the gym teacher. How do you feel?*

J: *Mad.*

MG: *Now sweep the mad feelings into the corner and talk to them kindly. Tell them you'll pay attention to them after school.*

(J: nods in agreement.)

MG: *Now tell me what you are seeing.*

J: *I'm not mad.*

MG: *Are you playing the game?*

J: *Yes.*

P.S. The gym teacher reported a great improvement in

cooperativeness.

The Story of Sam

When Sam first entered my ninth-grade reading class, he was able to read at only the third-grade level. My earliest memory of him was the time he tried to relate an incident to the class. I couldn't understand his story, because he was telling things out of sequence; for example, he would start in the middle and then perhaps tell the ending, followed by the beginning of the story, etc.

I stopped him and told him to tell me one thing at a time, while I wrote his sentences on the board. When he was through, I rearranged the sentences into a sequential order. After that, we were able to have an intelligible discussion about the incident.

As the class ended, Sam thanked me for helping him to speak in a clear manner. *"Now, because of this class, I can think more clearly about what I have to say in court next week. It was all mixed up in my mind. Thanks."*

In addition to learning to speak correctly, Sam learned to read better. He readily applied his phonics rules that I taught and by his sophomore year he could read almost anything with no errors. Sadly, however, by his senior year he appeared to have made very little emotional adjustment to life, and his chances for the future looked dim.

Sam Learns He Can Offend without Intention

One time, Sam asked permission to go to his locker at the beginning of class. I said OK. He came back quite a bit later.

MG: *You were gone a very long time.*

(Sam responded with body language that expressed anger.)

MG: *What was so terrible about what I said?*

Sam: *I messed up my leg in wrestling and couldn't walk fast.*

MG: *Did you think I knew that?*

Sam: *No.*

I took him through an exercise in which he imagined himself as the teacher in my place. After he mentally repeated the scene, he immediately acknowledged that he got the point.

Sam: *I been that way lately. Even this girl noticed it (i.e., the crossness).*

Hanging Out in the Hall

Sam had been staying out in the hall, socializing before class. He would ignore the bell and wait for me to call him in. I wrote him the following note:

Sam stayed out in the hall, well past the bell. Does he think it is the teacher's responsibility to call him into the room? If she doesn't call him, will he stay in the hall all period? What would he do if he were the teacher?

Does Sam think he is only four years old? A little child forgets to do things. He needs a bigger person to tell him what to do. If mother forgets to call him into the house and he stays out too late, it is mother's fault.

If mother forgets to wake up the four-year-old, and he is late to day care or nursery school, it is her fault. [Note: When Sam has been late to school, he would say that his mother didn't wake him on time.]

I bet Sam thinks it's the teacher's responsibility to call him into the room. If Sam were the teacher, and a student did not come into the room unless he was called, I wonder what Sam would think. I wonder how he would feel.

Subsequently, he stood *inside* the doorway while socializing.

Sam Heals His Pain from Wrestling

Sam came to class complaining of a pain in his neck from wrestling and told me the coach had said the pain would go away after he wrestled more. I described the difference, as I understood it, between Eastern martial arts such as *Aikido*, and Western martial arts such as boxing. I emphasized the importance of using the mind while doing exercises. This is done by visualizing the muscles, as in doing Yoga. Instead of taking the attitude that the muscles must become stressed and sore, I have found that a better way to exercise is to *pay attention* to how your muscles feel, and how they move. When this imagery becomes an integral part of the exercise, there is no soreness afterward.

After much urging, I convinced him to try using imagery now to heal himself. I had him visualize himself going through the wrestling exercises slowly and in great detail, allowing the muscles to rest frequently.

After three cycles of visualizing, the pain disappeared. Then the bell rang, and as he was walking out, I touched his shoulder and quietly said, *"Sam, tell me 'thank you.'"*

"Thanks," he said.

Since Sam was my student for both English *and* reading classes, he showed up again for fourth period. He was not feeling well. *"I need something to eat,"* he said.

I made him some *Miso Cup* soup from a package I kept in

my desk, using hot water from my thermos.

"Needs salt," he commented, but ate it all. *"I feel very full. Thank you."*

"Thanks again," he said while leaving.

Sam's Temper

While Sam had made great progress in his language skills since ninth grade (the previous year), his emotional behavior had worsened. During the current year, when the class was heatedly discussing an issue, Sam had his hand insistently in the air. I told him I would not interrupt someone else to let him talk, and that he would get his turn.

He became very angry, claiming that his hand was up earlier, and that I had called on Raul to speak instead of himself. The more he talked, the angrier he became, using some of those colorful current expressions. He finally *slammed* out of the room, allowing no one to say anything to him.

I wrote an MDO (Major Disciplinary Offense) to his vice principal with a note describing the incident and recommended a conference and detention instead of suspension. During his class the next day, I talked about temper. Later the vice-principal telephoned to say that he wanted to see us. The conference consisted of his scolding Sam and giving him a one-hour detention instead of suspension. At the end of the meeting, the V-P said, *"I want to hear later that you apologized to Mrs. Gifford."*

Outside the office I told Sam I was not comfortable with the idea of ordering someone to apologize. If an apology is ordered, it feels meaningless to me. For his part, Sam was burning with anger.

A short time later, he "cussed out" a teacher who asked to

see his ID upon encountering him in the hall. He was suspended for two days.

Note: It's possible that if the vice-principal had given Sam an opportunity to critique his behavior of the previous day, and we had discussed the incident as adults, Sam's resentful attitude might have changed to a more mature one.

Sam's Violence

I phoned the adjustment specialist to relate three violent incidents that Sam had described to the class during the week:

1. *As he told us about a fight at the East Hartford Cinema, he demonstrated how he would have "stomped on the head" of a kid from the other gang. When I commented that he could kill the boy, he answered, "It would be him or me. They would do that to me".*

2. *He said his mother hit him on the elbow with a metal pipe because he had his brother's head in a "head-lock." He was "going to kill" his brother for getting on his nerves. In response to my question, he said he loves his brother.*

3. *He said he can't come after school to work with me on his problems of violence and temper, because he works in* Stop and Shop *after school. He said he "almost killed a guy" at work who got on his nerves. Probably he meant he was tempted to, but restrained himself.*

The adjustment specialist said he'd speak with him and observe him. He suggested I might have Sam do relaxation exercises during free time if possible. I had suggested convening a *Planning Team* Meeting in the hope of getting him professional psychotherapy, but the adjustment specialist thought we should first try the school's resources.

Unfortunately, the school's resources proved to be incapable of helping Sam come to terms with his extreme anger and habits of violence. He continued getting into trouble until the end of his senior year. Such a waste of an otherwise talented and good person!

My Note to an Irate Sam

Dear Sam:

Yesterday you were so busy screaming at me that you didn't even listen when I tried to answer your question about why I wanted to have a meeting with your teachers. I will tell you now in this note:

I wanted to talk about how we could help you to get a better education, and how we could help you develop habits that would keep you out of trouble, and how we could help you grow into a young man who could succeed in college and make a successful and happy life for himself.

If you think you have to have a bad temper because your father or mother has one, I want you to know that you are mistaken. You can learn to be different. You can help it if you want to learn how. There are people who can teach you how to be mature and calm, but only if that is something you want.

Instead of treating me like an enemy, do you think that maybe I am someone you can trust? I would appreciate it if you would talk to me with kindness, because that's the way I talk to you.

If you don't want me to talk with teachers about improving your school life, just say so. I am not interested in forcing anything onto you.

I gave this note to Sam as he was leaving my class. The next time I saw him, he apologized and behaved in a more gentle and respectful manner. However, the meeting with his teachers never took place, since he did not indicate he wanted it. I wonder if it could have made a difference?

A Suggestion that Didn't Quite Work

Sam was too tired to attend to the lesson, and as we talked, he kept his head down on the desk. He said he'd been walking around the streets until three o'clock in the morning, but was unwilling to tell me why. I asked if he knew what could happen from such behavior, and he nodded "yes".

Then I remarked that the part of him that made him walk around at night was really trying to help. He agreed. So I suggested that maybe that same part could come up with an idea of something *else* he might do, besides walking around. He indicated that he heard and understood, but kept his head down, eyes closed.

I then worked with Carol on her lesson. After a few moments, Sam sat up and said, *"I know where the Hill Center is."*

When I looked puzzled, he said, *"Didn't you say I should go there?"*

"No."

"Then I must have dreamed it."

I offered the idea that the part of him that was trying to help had made the suggestion that he go there for counseling. He agreed, but when I asked when he planned to go, he said he didn't know.

"Tonight?" I asked suggestively. (I **should** have said, *"Will it be this week or next week?"* Milton Ericson would no doubt

have said something like that, and I was trying to adopt some of his wisdom, although not wisely enough, as it turned out.) He said he would be too busy tonight.

"When then?"

"I don't know."

As far as I know, he never went for counseling. I felt I had missed the boat on that one; the power of indirect suggestion can be fragile if not used well.

How to Lessen Bad Feelings: Experience Them; An Aikido Strategy

Many people feel pain and pretend that they do not feel anything. If, however, they are willing to admit to themselves that they are feeling it, an Aikido type of strategy can be a way to relieve the pain. By sitting quietly and allowing the pain to be present for twenty minutes, one often will find that at the end of that time, one is feeling much better.

Sam walked into second-period class and sat down at the back of the room, a miserable, angry look on his face. When invited to join in the classwork, he declined, saying he didn't feel like it today. After a few minutes, he said he wanted to go to Ms. G's room (adjustment specialist). I knew from experience that a lot of unpleasantness would be avoided by not arguing, but I told him I'd have to call first to get her permission.

Ms. G, it turned out, had her hands more than full with the *Human Dynamics* class. Her response to my message was, "Is he having a problem? Because I can't handle one more problem right now."

"Are you having a problem? Ms. G wants to know."

"No," he muttered. I returned to the phone to give his answer.

She asked, *"What does he want?"* I relayed the question. *"Nothing. Never mind. I'll stay here,"* without expression.

I said nothing and passed out papers, putting one on the empty desk beside him so that he could participate if he so decided.

After a short time he got up and walked to the door. I asked where he was going, and he sullenly indicated that he intended to walk around the corridors till he cooled off. I put the other students on automatic pilot, otherwise known as *"peer tutoring"*, and followed him out into the hall.

He refused to tell me what was wrong, answering *"no"* to each of my questions. No, nothing terrible had happened at home; no he wasn't upset over a girl; etc. He acknowledged that he was upset, however, but didn't really know why.

After he refused my offer to help him come to terms with his feelings, I told him that I didn't want him to get into trouble by wandering the halls. He looked extremely distressed, obviously close to tears. So I told him that it was OK to feel terrible, and that it might be good to stay with those feelings and respect them, even though he didn't know what they were about.

He remained silent, leaning against the wall, with alternating looks of pain and no-pain. I stayed silently with him. After perhaps fifteen minutes, he turned and walked back into the room and sat down. He looked a lot less stressed.

He didn't show up for his fourth-period class with me. Later, however, when I was out of the room (leaving the student teacher in charge), he came to explain his absence. Finding me gone, he dictated an explanatory note to the student teacher to give to me. The message indicated that he had to go somewhere to take care of a problem. I was impressed that he was conscientious enough to have come back to explain.

"I Hate to Read"

MG: *Sam, you need to make a choice as to whether you want to be a good person who helps people or a bad person who hurts people (dealing drugs, fighting, etc.)*

Sam: *The trouble is I hate to read, so I can't be what I want to be.*

MG: *I know how to help you be what you want.*

Sam: *But I hate to read.*

MG: *If you're not willing to do what you hate to do in order to learn, then I won't be able to help you.*

At this time, Sam was a sophomore. He had demonstrated that he now could read almost anything by applying the phonics instruction he'd learned the previous year. Unfortunately however, I had not yet discovered the power of special imagery strategies to help students read more easily and comfortably. In addition, it seemed that his greatest need now was for intensive psychotherapy and ongoing moral support. Unfortunately also, as already stated, the school system did not offer him such an option.

He spent a great deal of his junior year dozing or being otherwise inattentive. Consequently, he failed the year.

When he was a senior, I agreed to change his previous year's grade to a *D*, provided that he would work conscientiously for his new English teacher. He failed to keep the bargain.

Disappointment

When working with high school learning disabled students, especially those with emotional problems, we must be prepared for disappointments, in spite of the time and the caring that we invest in them. Such was the case when it came to my student Sam. Although he made great strides in learning to read, this achievement was not enough to save him from the streets. He, unfortunately, seemed to lack the critical requirement that most teen-agers need—namely, a strong supportive parent.

While Sam seems to care about right and wrong, it appears that his future does not look bright. The pull of easy money and undesirable friends, coupled with an unmet need for long-term psychological and moral support, were too much for him. He dropped out of school toward the close of his senior year. The following year he came to see me with the news that he had joined a gang. He also said that he was now the father of a baby and that the mother would have nothing to do with him..

I expressed my disappointment at his having joined a gang, and we both acknowledged that one could not get out of it without grave risk. He explained his actions by saying that he had joined because the gang was "family," a description I'd heard from others many times.

Could the supportive environment at a caring private boarding school have saved him? Probably only if it offered good psychological support.

Chapter Twelve

Discussing Values
in the Classroom

Does teaching about values have a place in a public school? Do we still believe that teachers should teach only "proven facts"? Times have changed greatly, and topics that once were the province only of the church and the home need now to be discussed in the school, since, sadly, many young people miss out on a strong relationship with both of these institutions.

Obviously there is a risk involved in discussing values, since not all teachers display wisdom and integrity. Nevertheless, it is a greater risk to allow the void to continue. Students, on the whole, can identify teachers who are out of line and speak with extreme bias.

I have found that most students, when presented objectively, respectfully, and with good humor with the varying views about ethics, religion, and sexual behavior, decide in favour of the respectful treatment of themselves and others, and ultimately make up their own minds.

What is dangerous to society and to young people is to allow them to grow up without good role models or without ever hearing an honest and informed discussion of all kinds of behavior. Too often, parents are unable to act as good role models. Today's television frequently serves to fill this vacuum with horrifying models for the unprepared viewer. I believe, therefore, that those teachers who feel comfortable doing so, should present fairly the various views of society, without necessarily identifying their own views. When I have included discussions of these topics in my classes, I have found, almost without exception, that the students participate with interest and judge with thoughtfulness.

On a related issue, what can a teacher do for a student who comes to class confused or upset about a current life problem? In a large mainstream class, the wisest course might be to allow the student to visit the school counselor.

I have found, however, that in a relatively small special ed class, it can be valuable for everyone if the student is willing to allow his situation to be used as a lesson, and, of course, if the teacher feels comfortable in this activity. Obviously, this lesson would necessitate the postponement of the orginally-planned one. The impromptu lesson would have the benefit of helping to develop communication skills in a meaningful situation, in addition to helping the troubled individual deal with a painful or confusing experience

Thus, we can have our cake and eat it too; i.e., we respect and address the needs of the troubled student. Then, when we go on to the planned lesson, the student will be better able to listen. Meanwhile the class has benefitted from a discussion of some of the anxieties, guilts, and dilemmas that accompany life, especially in adolescence.

Sometimes a student challenges me about spending class time on someone's personal problems. In such cases, I reply that it is more interesting to use real life situations to learn communication skills such as listening, expressing yourself, and thinking clearly. Without these skills, it is difficult to read in a meaningful manner. If you cannot make sense of what other people say, the chances are that it will be even more difficult for you to understand what you read.

I ask them, further, *"What is the ultimate purpose of learning to read?"* One answer is that it improves our chances for a happy life. At the same time, if you don't know how to get along with people, or have a good relationship with a spouse or partner, you're not likely to have a happy life, even if you *can* read. The students have no problem agreeing with that statement.

It is with this attitude that I present a number of discussions that my students and I have shared.

Attitudes Concerning Character, Money, Sexuality

Roger and Corman

Yesterday Roger asked if the word *bud* meant *seed*. From there the discussion progressed to human seed and reproduction.

Corman offered the comment that he was going to wait until marriage before having sex, and I said I believed that was a wise and mature attitude. Roger explained, somewhat defensively, that his older cousins were all sexually active, and that he was influenced by their example. I had the feeling that Corman's comment made a lot of sense to Roger.

The discussion then focused on the subject of trust and respect for other people, regardless of gender, race, or religion. Roger said that when he lived in the South, sometimes an individual would address him as *"boy,"* whereupon Roger would respond that he had a name, and he would be glad to tell it to them if they were interested. We talked about name-calling, and I recalled the time when a student had called Corman a *"nigger,"* to which Corman had responded, *"I may be black, but I'm not a nigger."*

I asked what they thought of people whose families and ancestors had been persecuted because of their religion or skin color, and then after they were legally entitled to fair treatment and respect, they took on the same attitudes as their persecutors, advocating hatred of different races or religions. At this, Corman said, *"That's the* Nation of Islam; *that's how* **they** *are."*

As the bell rang, Roger said he believed that all people should get together as one and live in peace and mutual respect. He added that that was the basis of his religious feelings. Corman agreed wholeheartedly.

Caleb and Roger

Caleb and Roger were both in my science class. We often discussed values and relationships. Caleb repeatedly declared that money was the highest and only value. Roger would respond in a serious and respectful way, expressing his own opposite views. I was disappointed that Roger's attitude of respect towards others seemed to make no impression upon Caleb.

In our discussions of human relations, Roger seemed to step out of character on one subject: homosexuality. The previous year, when the subject had first come up, he had said he would gladly join in beating up gays if the opportunity arose. There followed discussions of why some people are gay and others are heterosexual. Our science lessons dealt with human sexuality, and when the students showed an interest in pursuing the subject of gays and lesbians, I was able to present various views.

At one point I mentioned that a large percentage of teenage homosexuals commit suicide. Roger said that's what he would do if he discovered he were gay. As time went on, however, he seemed to have modified his murderous approach, as the following essay illustrates:

My Perfect World [as dictated by Roger]

I would get rid of all the gangs. I would throw all the gang members in jail or give all of them guns and put them in a big open field and let them shoot at each other.

I will open a center for young kids to prevent gangs, so little kids can play basketball, football, and other types of sports.

I would put the gays in an island alone, so then they could do what they want. Then if they make a pass at somebody, it would not be someone who was not gay.

To prevent passes at straight people, I would tell them to keep your sex life to yourself. Open up gay bars for them, if they stay here [instead of on the island.]

If a man or woman makes a pass at someone, tell him or her that you don't like them and to go away. If they don't go away, file a suit for harassment.

If a gay guy made a pass, I would rather hit him than put him in jail.

The Story of Caleb—
A Sociopath in Tenth Grade?

Teacher: "How come you are suddenly so nasty to Elwood, when you were practically inseparable before?"

Caleb: "Oh I just used him for a while, and now I don't need him any more, so I threw him away."

This was the conversation that a colleague had with one of our mutual students. When she told me about it, I began to understand some things about Caleb's behavior that had puzzled me. I have met possibly two people in my life whose behavior was "sociopathic," and Caleb seemed to be a third.

When he entered my class, one of the first things he said to me was that he owned a *Subaru Legacy*, a fact which meant nothing to me, except that I was evidently supposed to be impressed.

In class discussions, he seemed more sophisticated than his classmates, except when it came to understanding feelings of respect. Usually he was courteous, but, on occasion, if I had to remind him of the consequences of an undesirable behavior, his response would be a quiet and supercilious, "Oh really?" This in itself is not so unusual, but together with his calm self-control and his interest in learning to read better, it seemed incongruous.

One time he commented that my old metal minute-timer was "a piece of junk," and asked why I didn't get a new one.

I replied that some of us have to work for our money. "Where do you get yours?" I asked. He didn't answer.

Another time I spoke with him privately, saying that I thought he was not like the other students. I started to say,

"You don't seem to have feelings of...". He finished what he thought I was going to say, by supplying the word *"love?"*

"Actually, I was going to say 'kindness,'" I replied. *"When you watch TV and see a little child suffering or being tortured, do you feel bad?"*

He responded with genuine interest, *"No, I enjoy it."* He seemed surprised and validated by my understanding and interest.

After his "friendship" with Elwood had ended, I encountered Caleb in the corridor with another boy, Juan. When I asked to see their passes, Caleb ignored my question and said earnestly that he needed to use a phone and didn't know where to find one. I told him he was to see his vice-principal about that, but Juan was to remain with me. They refused to part, so I had the security guard take them both upstairs to the vice-principal's office.

Later, I told Juan that Caleb was using him for what he could get out of him, and then would "throw him away" as he had done to Elwood. Caleb smirked as he listened. I couldn't tell if he was embarrassed or proud.

A few days later, I encountered a repeat of the corridor episode, only this time the "patsy" with Caleb was yet another ninth-grader.

Caleb Describes His Values

We were discussing money and values in class. Caleb said he wouldn't care if he had no friends or family, as long as he had money. In discussing feelings, he said he'd never felt sad or happy. He has felt anger, and one time he felt fear. That was when he was driving his car with a young boy in the passenger's seat. When he had to slam on the brake, the boy hit his head on the dashboard and pretended to be unconscious. Caleb at first believed he *was* unconscious and felt frightened, because he thought the boy might sue him.

Caleb and Pedro

I talked with Caleb and Pedro about what I thought each of them would wish for, if they could get a magic wish. These were the thoughts I expressed:

To Caleb: "Everyone would look up to you and admire and obey you, because you would have so much money and power. Then you would feel that you are a very important person, because they say so."

Caleb said that I was correct.

To Pedro my guess was that he wished he could read and write better. He disagreed, saying, "I wish people would leave me alone and not bother me so much."

When we discussed *My Perfect World*, Caleb said, *"In my perfect world, I own everything. There are no men, and the women all have to do what I say."*

I replied, *"No, you're not present in this world. So what would the perfect world be?"*

He then said, *"There would be no weapons. If people had a problem, they could go somewhere and talk it out, like in elementary school. There would be no need for money, etc."*

I then assigned them to write on this subject. The following is Caleb's essay:

The World I Love

My idea of a perfct world would be if they wear [were] no guns in the world and no money. And every body loved each other like brother and sister and every body would help eash other grow food on farms. And thir would be planty of animals the animals wont be scared from the humens.

If their was money thier would be fighting over it becous some people kill other people for mony. A lot of people get muded [mugged] for their mony. In this world they would thrad [trade] crops, sheep, and fruits and more. If their was a fight the people wood stop and talk it over. and everbody wuld be treted equle nobody would hat[e] no one.

Comment: This essay indicated to me that, in spite of Caleb's apparent lack of feelings of respect and love, he nevertheless had an innate *potential* for these feelings. I believe that the note he wrote in my *Retirement Book* showed feelings of appreciation. (See the last episode about Caleb.)

Report of Caleb's Behavior
(This is a Copy of a Note I Sent to Caleb's Counselor.)

Wed. 2/16
During reading class (oral reading in pairs, with student teacher observing) Caleb leaned across another student's desk and asked Berto if he would like to read, knowing full well that Berto couldn't read and never participated in the lesson. (Berto is retarded and was wrongly scheduled into the class.) His obvious purpose was to humiliate Berto.

Thurs. 2/17
He came tardy to science class without a pass. He re-

fused detention. I gave him an MDO.

> *Tues. 2/22*
> *He came to second period and sat reading a magazine, ignoring me when I told the students to get their books out. When I asked why he was ignoring me, he said he had to see something and continued perusing it. I asked if he knew a more appropriate way to respond, and he ignored me. After a couple of minutes, he got up and started looking for his book.*
>
> *I instructed the four students who were present to work together in pairs. Caleb proceeded to ignore me and to work on his own, while Elwood kept looking toward him for cooperation.*
>
> *I had announced that if they failed to cooperate as instructed, they would get zero's. I then told Elwood he could work with me and I would read the questions aloud to him. Elwood got 100. I refused to correct Caleb's paper. The unpleasant matter soon ended with the sounding of the bell.*

Note: The counselor told me that Caleb was constantly being suspended last year, and that his father had sadly said that his son was "no good."

Further Examples of Caleb's Character

Although Caleb took obvious pleasure in seeing other people hurt, he did not himself act physically violent. This characteristic was illustrated by the following episode that took place a few days after I had sent the note to Caleb's counselor:

Elwood came into class one day, very upset over an incident that had taken place in his previous class. It seems he had been at the teacher's desk, waiting to have his work checked. The teacher's back was toward him while he waited, and meanwhile another boy punched Elwood with no provocation. Then the boy turned to Caleb and said, *"Should I hit him again?"* whereupon, according to the report of Torrie (who had witnessed the incident), Caleb replied, *"No, wait till later."*

I Try to Change Caleb's Outlook

I wondered if Caleb could be called a *sociopath*. Although I'd heard that there is no known way to change such a person, I nevertheless began to get an idea. Perhaps I could persuade him to *behave* differently. Even though he enjoyed using and hurting people, it was possible that he might have the capacity to realize that eventually others would recognize what kind of a person he was, and he would thus never get the admiration he was looking for. If, on the other hand, he chose to *act* like other people, instead of lying and hurting others, he might eventually get the recognition and respect that he valued. In this daydream I recognized that I would probably fail, but I couldn't give up trying. My opportunity came a few months later.

We were discussing dating and the importance of money on a date. Caleb said it was important to have money, because then the girl would be impressed. Roger disagreed, indicating that if that was all the girl was interested in, then he wouldn't be interested in *her*.

We talked about feelings of love and caring, and Caleb said that he does not have those feelings. He asserted that he valued only money and power.

Roger then said to him seriously, *"I feel sorry for you. You don't know what you're missing in life. It's like you have an empty life."* [Note: At a previous time, however, Caleb had revealed that he had a sister who was retarded, and that he felt bad for her. That was my only glimpse of his ability to care about someone.]

I then proceeded to tell them the story of a family I knew who behaved as though they shared the same beliefs as Caleb:

A very wealthy family bought a summer house in a small beach community. The neighbors were friendly and welcomed the new family, although most of them thought it was unfortunate that the newcomers bragged about how rich they were. In time, people realized that their new neighbors could not be trusted. For example, if someone refused to do what the new neighbors wanted, they could become dangerous. In one case, the adult son broke into the summer home of a family who had refused to sell him their house. He stole an expensive appliance, and then the father even bragged to some people about having it! (Of course he didn't actually say his son had stolen it.)

Naturally, most of the people learned to avoid them. The wealthy family felt hurt and couldn't understand why they were disliked. Soon they put their house up for sale, but they asked so much money that no one would buy it.

After finishing the story, I wrote the word *sociopath* on the board, explaining that the suffix *path* meant *sick*, while *socio* referred to *people* or *society*. *Sociopath*, therefore, meant someone who had an attitude toward people that most of us regard as sick.

Caleb listened intently, but made no comment. However,

after several other discussions, his own behavior began to change a little. Gone were the supercilious replies, and even the smirking when someone was embarrrassed. I don't believe that his *feelings* necessarily changed, but at least he seemed to be putting on a more decent act.

My Advice to Caleb

Caleb reminds me of the little girl in the nursery rhyme: When he's good, he's very, very good, and when he's bad he's horrid.

In time, he began behaving in a more respectful and helpful way. He made significant progress in spelling, and his reading improved dramatically. He caught on to explanations and phonics rules quickly and showed promise of ultimately being able to function in mainstream classes.

After class one day, I asked him to stay for a few minutes, and I gave him some advice about his future. It went something like this:

*"I know that the most important values for you are money, power, and to be respected." He nodded in agreement. "It's possible that even though you're not in touch with feelings of kindness, those feelings might be hidden from your awareness. Now, even if you don't **feel** respectful and kind, it might be a good idea to **behave** as though you did. In that way, people will believe good things about you, and because you are smart, you have a good chance to be successful and respected. If you can be trusted, you might get a good job and be able to prove that you have ability.   BUT—if you think you can do nasty things once in a while, or lie and steal, you can be sure that someone will recognize it, and that will be the end of your good reputation.*

So if you want to have a good life, you're going to have to act honest and straight, no matter how you feel."

He listened attentively, and as I finished, a fleeting smile crossed his face. He thanked me as he left.

Might he have taken me seriously? He evidently decided to apply my advice, because the next time I saw Caleb, he entered the classroom in a quiet and gentlemanly manner, sat down and immediately took out his work, waiting for the class to begin. Throughout the lesson he behaved seriously and respectfully, in spite of occasional disruptions or silliness by some other students. I was amazed at his completely mature aspect, and I found myself feeling warm toward him in spite of his past behavior.

I'm happy to say that his respectful and serious behavior continued till the end of school. It felt like a miracle!

*Note: Some readers may feel that I was advising Caleb to be hypocritical. However, the alternative—i.e., to continue to be nasty—is certainly not acceptable. It would seem rather fruitless to advise someone to **feel** kind and generous. I tell my students that I don't blame anyone for feelings they may have; only for acting on those feelings in a hurtful way. Furthermore, there is always the hope that, just as good feelings can influence behavior, so, too, might good behavior influence feelings.*

Caleb's Final Essay

"The things that I did in Mrs. G. Rroom.
The things that [I] did this year wher [were] some time fun times and some bad. Whe[we] learnd a lot of reding skills and vowels. I remember when we wer talking about the milk

and what they did to it [injecting cows with bovine growth hormone] *now that was one of the fun thing we did. and their were time when we talked about religion and some times we would argue about it.* [Note from Mrs. G: I never argued, but tried to steer them to respect each other's views.]

"What activities were good.
The activities that wher good wher when we did mind [mental] *spelling and when we did imagery. What did you lean I learned that it was veary heltey [healthy] for the mind and you also feel good right after we wher done.*

"The bad thing that I remberd
The bad thing that I rembmer wher when I got lots of M.d.o.s [vice-principal's detention] *and when I didn't whant to lesson* [listen] *to the teacher. I remember when I had to go to see Mrs. Taylor and some times she would give me a brake. But some time she didn't give me a brake She would S.S.P. me. or give me friday academy.* [Detention]

OH I almost forgot about the time when we had that sudent teacher Mr. Brown He gave me a hand some times. I thing that he will become a good teacher wher ever he is. and I remember Mrs. More[Moore] *now that was some of the day's that were very good. She was always helpful to me an the others I sure she will be fun teacher to have. But the things that I learnd the most was from Mrs. Gifford She always be a grate teacher.*

"If I could do the year over
if I could do the year over I would start biy soming [coming] *to school every day and pay more attention. And get better grades."*

Caleb Signs My Friendship (Retirement) Book

The teachers in my department gave me a *Friendship Book* when I was planning to retire. It was like an autograph book, and when Caleb saw the book on my desk, he wrote the following message in it:

Dear Mrs. Gifford,
I hope that you have a wondeful life and be verry success-
ful. You will never be forgot and I hope in the futer I can
bumb [bump] in to you I thank you for the things you did

P.S. The following year (when I was retired) Caleb's counselor told me that Caleb was acting much more respect-fully, but at the same time was discouraged and depressed. A little later in the year I learned that he had quit school. I tried to contact him but was unsuccessful. I feel concern for his well-being, and can only hope that he will be all right.

Section Three

Communications

Chapter Thirteen

Communication with Colleagues

To: Special Ed Staff
Re: Early Dismissal Jobs for Special Ed Students

I am requesting an urgent meeting this week of all Special Ed staff. It is becoming very apparent that we need some strictly enforced rules for those of our students who leave school early to go to a job.

One of my student's grades has dropped from A to D, and another student's has plummeted from A to F. The latter student seems to have lost all interest in school and is frequently absent. This is especially unfortunate as he is quite intelligent and would have a good chance of success in college.

Feedback anyone?

Millie

cc: H (Vice Principal)

Note: The vice-principal came to the meeting, and shortly thereafter the two boys dropped their after-school jobs. Their grades went back up.

More Communication with Colleagues

A Rude and Uncooperative Student

To: E. R. (Counselor)
From: Mildred Gifford, Skills Lab Teacher
Report on Eddie

Eddie refuses to cooperate in class. He has told me that my rule against chatting is stupid, and he refuses to accept supervision and help, insisting upon using skills lab as a combination study hall/social time.

It is foolish for him to remain in skills lab and get an F, when the whole purpose is to help him succeed in the mainstream. Perhaps a human dynamics class would be more meaningful, since it's his attitude that appears to be an obstacle to academic success.

I am attaching reports from three teachers. All of them complained about his attitude and chatting during class.

Any help or feedback would be appreciated.

Thank you.
Mildred Gifford

cc: H [Vice-principal]
E [Human Dynamics Teacher]

Note: The next day Eddie came into my room and courteously said hello. He responded to my offer of help by showing me his social studies problems and proceeded to work industriously all period.

Eddie's Essay Exam

Well I think that what Mrs. Gifford and I talk made a lot of sence. Some were good like what she told me to think or make a movie how I am going to act on Tuesday and I love it. Its true I'm a stubborn person. I need to work on this more because if I work on it I would have a better friend with Mrs. Gifford and I would feel better. I thank her for what she did today I feel much better.

I think that what we talked about it could help me alot like just comming and say hi and straight to the homework. I feel much better if this would work. I think I could make it work. I'll try not to talk, gossip or even chatt with Olga or anybody else. I'll try to coroperate with everything.

This paper would be of great help to me and to Mrs. Gifford I thank you For everything.

I think its true what Mrs. Gifford said that a true Christian must respect and its true I try but it doesn't work, is something inside of me that wants to be disrespectful and their another one that does want to be respectful and they fight everyday they fight its like a war or something. See what I'm trying to say if I say something please forgive and If you could try to help me. Ever since I got into Church I loved it it was good great and happiness but when I got to this class I would be silly. Fooling around and acting immature. I said to myself that a Christian suppose to have manner and show what a true Christian is. I'm going to try to be more respectful and show what a true Christian is.

Note: Eddie and I had been having trouble understanding

each other, and I was angry with his silly and often uncooperative behavior. After the lesson that he describes above, we both felt better about each other, and his behavior became more respectful.

Memo about Current Ninth-Graders

To: Special Ed Teachers
From: Millie Gifford
Re: A Different Crop of Ninth Graders

   G just turned sixteen, but his way of speaking often sounds like an unhappy six-year-old. His behavior is not unusual for this year's crop of ninth-graders. He usually comes into the room, sits at the back of the class, and puts his head down on the desk. Sometimes he will warn me that he's not going to do any work, or that he's angry about one thing or another. Like many of his peers, he can take offense at the most harmless remark from another student.

   Many of the students obviously feel so terrible so much of the time, that they hear an insult even when none is given. Then they respond defensively and offensively, to one degree or another. We teachers need to be alert to these sudden flare-ups. It is easy for a big argument or even a fight to erupt from the silliest of remarks. We all know of too many unfortunate incidents that have occurred already.

   It's obvious that suspension is no longer the answer to these problems. We need to find a meaningful way to address the smoldering deep inside. Is there a way we can provide for daily attention to their emotional needs? It is obvious that not all of the students who need it can be accommodated by the Human Dynamics classes. However, if we continue to expect these students to attend classes as usual, and if we neglect to come up with some additional ways of dealing with the situation, we can expect the problems only to get worse. Since the system's resources are obviously too strained to get many kids adequate help, I believe that we teachers may want to try to come up with ideas for dealing with the situation. Perhaps we can apply strategies learned from the Substance Abuse Prevention Program or any other ideas you may suggest.

I am willing to meet with staff any time to brainstorm for solutions. I understand that there is no special program planned for this Thursday's Inservice. If you are interested, let's plan to meet at 1:00 in room 168.

Note: Only one teacher showed up. Two others expressed regrets that they had a previous commitment. I had hoped that someone would pick up the initiative, since I felt discouraged and gave up. Unfortunately, we're all so busy that I can't blame anyone else for this idea's not going anywhere. I just didn't summon the energy to push it further.

Chapter Fourteen

Feedback from Students

Max's Feedback

The paper that follows was written by Max as part of the exam he took at the end of the school year.

> *This year was easy but helpful at the same time. Some of the stuff you tought me I already know, but most of it was interesting. You tought me vowel sounds I didn't know, the meaning of some words. You tought me how to focus my sees [eyes] when I read and how to use imagery. Letting us teach the class was fun and you gave us a brack [break] witch was also fun. Lots of things you tought me I can not rememeber but I know it was a interesting year.*

Max was an average student before the student teacher took over the class. After she began teaching, however, he began to slouch in his seat and refused to cooperate or pay attention. When I asked him why his behavior had changed, he responded with a mumble and a shrug.

Finally I decided to take over the class again and switched

to a different book. Max's attitude immediately changed. He began paying attention, doing his homework faithfully, and in general, became a model student. I didn't know if he had been uncooperative earlier because of the student teacher or because the work had become boring. However, when I switched back to the original program, his model behavior continued, and his reading skills showed significant gains.

Marian's Junior Year Feedback

I believe we should schedule students into LD classes according to skills level, not grade level. The following feedback from Marian illustrates the point:

My experience in this class was quite very different from the last 2 years I've been here. this year was easier and even though we had sometimes our disagreement I still enjoyed being here. I sometimes found the class a little boring but that was becouse I knew everything. I am hoping that next year I can be in a higher level so I dont have to be bored and learn something knew. These past 3 years I have learned alot about using my mine and thinking. And I thank you very much. I hope this summer you really enjoy your self!

Have a great summer.

P.S. I recommended that Marian be scheduled into a mainstream remedial reading class for her senior year. It worked out well.

Feedback from Alan

To enhance comprehension and memory, I would have the

students make a mental movie of each sentence or event as they read along. Then, when answering questions about a story, they would look into their own memory to find the answers, instead of going back to the text and copying the answers verbatim — robot style. This is what Alan was referring to when he wrote the fourth sentence in his feedback below. Although the sentences sound disconnected, he was obviously writing answers to questions that I had listed on the board, such as *what was helpful this year?* etc.

The morghographs [morphographs] was very helpful. The syllables was ok. It was a little borning. I enjoy when you help us think back of words look back in our mind. By readind the stories about the wolf hunting for some food. The direct Instruction was very very hard.

Nelson's Paragraph

What is useful in this class is the ways you teach people how too think. One thinx that I learned is this class is how to think better. Like everytime I think of something I picture it in my brain. That helps me to remine my self about what I had to do.

Feedback from Ivan

When I first went into Mrs. Gifford's class I thought she was crazy. Now that I know her things are not crazy any more. We see things in our minds. We also can get rid of headaches and other pains. We do lots of mind work and visualization work too. When someone in our class have things wrong with them we help them. We try to put our selves in thier shose. We try to see them in our minds doing well. Some times the person feels better. We also read lots of stories. Some stories are crazy but some are not. After a while stories get crazyer and wilder. I enjoy being in this class. Thank you for your help.

Feedback from Carl

1. The imagery was very helpful to me.
2. I learned how to read more words.
3. The ending of words was boring.
4. Nothing was hard to me.
5. The imaagery was fun.
6. If you teach more imagery next year. [Answer to "how could it be better?"]

Feedback from Kenneth

This year in your class I learned a lot about mophgraphs and what words mean. I learned how to think a word out if I don't know how to spell a word. I would close my eyes and try to see the word in my mind.

What I liked about this class is if any of us in the class have a problem we could go to you and by the end of the class our problem would either be solve or almost solved. like when Sep use to come in class and say something happened at his house you Mrs Gifford would help him or anybody else that would need help with a problem. That's what I like about this English class.

I would like to change, when Mrs Gifford is helping us with our problem, and we want to say something you would take long for us to get to say something else.

[I think he meant that Mrs. G should talk less and give the students a chance to talk more!!]

Feedback from Nicholas

Nicholas usually did his work in a hurry and never seemed to have the patience to check it. Obviously he failed to proof-read his paragraph carefully (as instructed), since he didn't catch the incomplete sentence about "subs".

The things that was the most helpful was the theacher that was teaching me. I Learned how to Sound out words that I would have problems with. I Learned how to read better. The things that are boring is when she sits there and tells you things about yourself. The things that were hard was the test. The times when we had subs. It could be better the next time if I sit down and do my work.

Feedback from Tabby

What had stop me form doing better is [in] *this class is that some people wood start taltking and I wood get so comfla* [confused] *that I wood just stop. And then it just get vary hard trying to get lack* [back] *on the subjet so that I wood just stop. But the moust* [most] *helpul think* [thing] *that real* [really] *help me was the look* [books] *and maby we cold* [could] *of had want up sone* [some] *nore* [more] *looks* [books] *but that ways* [was] *ok. I also lean* [learn] *how to sown out my world* [words] *vary very good. But the aney* [only] *thinking* [thing] *the* [that] *was realy realy boring was when we had to do saun* [sounds] *like aeiou say* [stuff] *like that. other whyz* [otherwise] *the class was a-o-k. Some of the work was ezes* [easy] *and some of it ways haard. But I did enjoy when the ticher shold* [showed] *us how to not feedback when one of the classneat* [classmates] *want* [wanted] *to start terbl* [trouble]. *But it maby can be etter* [better] *next tine if the class wood has kids that wood be more moceore* [mature]. *But maby if Mrs. Gifford wood also tack* [take] *the class on tirp* [trips] *to the liberyey and maybe the class wood has* [have] *a better way to leorn.*

Feedback fromTeresa

This year we did all kind of thinking [things] *like getting to talk to the teacher about all kind of thing even when we was haveing porblem with thing* [things] *that was happen* [happening] *to us at home or even on the street or it could of been in school.*

The activities we did that was fun was when we would talk as a grope [group] *it is real good to talk in a grope because people would get a chans to know you better and will start to understand you.*

I would not say that eney [any] *activities was bad. It had to be some one in the gurpe* [group] *to mess up the activities but most of the time it was fun all the time. I would not say it out lould* [loud] *but it was fun.*

But I did learn how to read some world [words] *that I thought*

I would never learn how to read. And I allso learn how to get along with other [others] and keep my self coom [calm]. Because at one time it was very hard for me to do that. When I came to Mis Gifford class I know [knew] thing [things] was going to chang with me. When I come [came] in I real [really] did not know how to do eney things but now if I was to walk out I would know how to read what some one have gave me to read.

And if I could do this year over agan the thing that I would of changed would be all the day [days] I miss out of school. I would chang the class and requiss [require] for it to be bigger so that other kids would be abel to come in and began some thing new. And then in that way if some of the old kids that us [used] to be in this class would of said that they wish that they could start to understand that it was fun and they could just amagent [imagine] all the fun that it would be and I only whis [wish] that all of the kids that was kick out or even drop out would of got ther self to gether because they just don't know what kind of techer that they mess [miss] out this year. And the years of 93-94 I will never fairget.

Feedback from Jose

My frist experience when I came to mod II was not good becances [because] the teacher was alway taking [talking] To us like if we were little kids but as the years [year] want on she become better at taking to Us as people not little kids But I got bad in class with Mis G. than I started to think That if I wanted to pass I got to be good in class so I started being good Mis G. got along Very will with me and than that whan

I started to be bad in class agan it seem that I let Mis G. down but I hope she doe's [doesn't] get a studen as bad as me!

P.S. Mis G. I thank you for being ther for [me] but I know I wasn't ther for You You are a good teacher and don't let anyone tell you wrong have a nice and piceful summer.

Love

Your studnen

Jose J.

Terrie's Feedback

I think the morphelgrah was helpful for the class because i think some people was doing good on morphelgraph. The ation [suffix] was bornig [boring]. I am not saying that because I didn't partespant [participate]. if I would of caught on it may of not be boring.

On the days when we talked about what was going on in the world that was fun. [It could have been better] if we will [would] have a sealtion [section?] on talking about importint [things]. learn [learning] the ation [suffix] was kind of hard if i had of tryed it may of not have been hard.

Tom's Feedback

1. What did you learn this year in my class?
   I learn to read Better and write Better and some time be good. But I still need work.

2. *What did you 1ike about this class?*
    I like about this class becouse it was differint then the ather classes.

3. *What would you like to change about this class?*
    I not like to change nothin about this class but I will have to learn to conto [control] *my alatod* [attitude].

Feedback from Ileana

1. *In this class I learned when the teacher is talking and teaching, She fills awful when you don't won't* [want] *to learn what she teaches.*

2. *I like when you going to explain the vowels, like the Captain C.*

3. *I don't have anything to change I just like that you keep on helping us the way you teach!*

Colman's Feedback

The first time I want [went] *to my new mod 2 class, for me it was not strang* [strange]. *I know everyone in the classroom The teacher is my old time homeroom teacher in room 206. She is a nice lady She teach very good, take time to go over things whit you. The kids I know well, some times we gate* [get] *out of hand with the tacher and that is not right.*

Tony's Feedback

The teacher in our class talked to us about how to do better in class. Like to be on time and things like that my bigest problem is to be on time to class. The way I thing that I will be on time to class is when I come out of my fourth period class. I would come to my class with out stoping to talk to my friends or do other things like going to my locker. I would Just come to class so I could be on time. That is what I think I should do to be to class on time. Or I should say to myself that I should be somewhere and this is not the place I should be and to get there before the bell rings so I would be on time so the teacher would not have anything to say but Hi not why are you late for class.

Postscripts

Lessons I've Learned in School

1. It doesn't pay to yell at kids.
   It boomerangs.

2. It doesn't pay to get insulted and let them know it.
   It boomerangs.

3. It doesn't pay to let them know I've lost my cool.
   I end up feeling foolish.
   It boomerangs.

4. None of the above is always true.
   Generalizations boomerang.

So What Does Pay?

As soon as I become aware of
insolence
non-compliance
rudeness
unnecessary tardiness

DEAL WITH IT IMMEDIATELY!

I Wish I Had Reached Them All

I realize that, each year, there were some students I paid less attention to than others because of the limited amount of extra time and energy that could be stolen from planning time, lunch time, and after-school hours. My conscience is somewhat eased when I realize that another teacher will befriend the student whom I may have overlooked. Fortunately, teachers differ from one another as much as students do.

"Individualize"

One of the first *shoulds* that a person learns when studying special education is that the learning disabled child should have her lessons *individualized*. Sometimes the colleges teach prospective teachers very little about *how* to individualize, beyond the idea, perhaps, that students may work in workbooks at their own pace.

A more meaningful way of "individualizing" is to label a child according to his individual strengths and weaknesses. For example, the child is labeled a *visual, auditory* or *kinesthetic learner*. Following this model, the teacher creates separate visual, auditory, and kinesthetic programs to accommodate each learning style. Dr. Joan Smith, in her book *You Don't Have to Be Dyslexic* describes in detail how this can be done.

Since the teacher training that I received mentioned concepts and terminology, but omitted teaching us the technology, I developed my own way of individualizing. Rather than consciously teaching through the learning style of individual students, I found it more meaningful to teach mostly in a whole-group interactive manner. My experience was that in order to be able to read easily and with comprehension, almost every student needs to learn to visualize, even if it's not her strong learning style.

While it does makes sense to take advantage of the student's strong modality, *it is also important to build up the deficient skills*. Students need to be able to understand language that they hear **and** see. I found that, regardless of whether it's the auditory or visual area that is weak, the use of pertinent visualization strategies can help remediate the situation. For example, there are some people who remember what they hear but have great difficulty visually perceiving printed words. What such students need are visualization strategies to enable them to *see* the words accurately.

On the other hand, there are people who have the opposite problem. For example they may be unable to discriminate between or remember the difference between two specific sounds, such as the short sounds of the vowels *e* and *i*. In this case, we say they have an *auditory* discrimination problem. Here I would use strategies that employ their visual and kinesthetic abilities to help them develop the deficient auditory skills. (For example, I might use a chart that illustrates the size of the jaw opening for each sound, and have the student place a hand under his jaw to feel and compare how wide the jaw needs to open for making each sound.)

For students with auditory memory problems, the solution is much simpler. If they visualize the meaning of each sentence immediately upon hearing it, their memory problem disappears.

The teaching of ***content*** courses, such as history or science, may be expedited by presenting the material through the student's strongest channel. Even here, however, if the teacher leads the students through a process of visualizing the historical scene or of imaging the charts and diagrams, the chances for the students to understand and remember the material will significantly improve.

What do the other students do while I am working alone with a single individual? Depending upon the situation, I might give the others individual worksheets as follow-up and reinforcement for the group lesson. They work either singly or with a partner .

Often, however, the entire class may participate in the remedial exercise. While LD students vary in their degree of skills development, most of them benefit from exercises to improve the skills of sequencing, memory, vocabulary, concepts, etc.

I believe that, in special ed reading classes where there is minimal interaction between and among the teacher and the class members, very little learning takes place. My experience is that effective lessons are taught between teacher and students, not between students and workbooks. Worksheets are useful for providing follow-up practice and drill *after* the interactive lesson has been taught.

Individualization further requires that, before working with a new student, the teacher must determine which skills the student needs to develop, and which phonemes [letter-sound relationships] he does not understand.

Until meaningful individualized instruction becomes more common, and until more effective programs and strategies are used, we shall continue to be dismayed that so many illiterate people are graduating from our high schools every year.

TV and Learning Disabilities

There is much talk about the harmful effects of television violence upon young people. We seldom hear about the potential harm extensive viewing may have upon *language facility* in a child who is relatively non-verbal to begin with.

What concerns me is the loss of time available for conversation, or listening to stories. This type of child needs to be encouraged to *visualize* what he or she hears. Television stories actually prevent the viewer from converting the story into mental pictures, since the pictures are already presented for the child *out there;* i.e., on the screen. Children who are disposed to dyslexia or learning disabilities do not automatically convert language into corresponding mental pictures (something that most people do unconsciously). Therefore, such children should be helped to develop the habit of visualizing what they hear. This might be accomplished through games, riddles, rewards, or explicit suggestion.

For example, if the child is requested to bring a pen, the red book, and a ruler from the other room, he will forget what he was supposed to bring. If, however, he is told to see the items in his mind as the request is being made, he will perform the task with no problem.

I am reminded of my severely language-handicapped student, Mike, who would forget what we were talking about even in the middle of a discussion which interested him. One time he asked how I had learned to talk "civilized." I wasn't quite sure what he meant, but I responded by asking if his family talked together very much. His answer was classic: "It depends what's on."

Bi-Lingual Special Ed Reading Program

Some pedagogical literature suggests that bilingual students should learn to read first in their dominant language in order to have a sound foundation for reading in English. When it comes to mainstream children, I have no opinion regarding this conclusion.

Even though this is an emotional and politically loaded subject, I must say that my experience with learning disabled students has led me to a different conclusion.

The learning disabled are deficient in the underlying skills needed for language proficiency, and one of these skills is awareness of the separate sounds in a word.

Especially troublesome for them when first learning to read is the critical need, not only to **hear** separate sounds within words, but also to remember the relationships between the sounds and their corresponding letters. Spanish and English have the same general alphabet and many similar sounds, but trouble arises because many of these same sounds, especially the vowels, are represented by different letters in each language. For example, in English the *long i* sound is written with the letter *i*, while in Spanish it is written *ai*. The *long e* sound in English uses the letter *e*, while in Spanish it is written *i*.

Similarly, there is confusion between the *short* sounds of the English *a* and *o*. What would be spelled with an *o* in English, is spelled with an *a* in Spanish. My students who have been taught to read Spanish before English repeatedly read *hot* for *hat*, *beat* for *bit*, etc. The problem is not so much that the pronunciation is incorrect, but that the *meaning* is wrong. These are examples of the frustrations that their mono-lingual peers are spared. They encounter further difficulty in remembering the differences between the sounds of *sh* and *ch*, *d* and *t*, etc.

Because of these differences, unnecessary confusion is generated for a child who already has severe problems with language. As a result, these bilingual students are prevented from progressing as rapidly as they should, and sometimes become so frustrated that they develop negative behaviors, or they drop out of school.

The reality is that our "learning disabled" population en-counters excessive and unnecessary difficulty in learning to read English if they have been taught to read Spanish first. They'd have a better chance at reading both languages rea-sonably well if **English** were taught first. Spanish is still rec-ognizable when read with English letter-sounds. For example, if a reader mispronounces the Spanish word *casa* with the "a" sound as in "fat", the meaning will still be understand-able, or at least it won't be confused with an entirely differ-ent word. Since Spanish does not have words with this short *a* sound, there will be no ambiguity.

I had one bilingual student who expressed great anger at having been forced (according to his report) to remain in bilingual classes his entire school career until ninth grade.

As of this writing, the issue is so emotionally loaded that many otherwise fine educators refuse even to consider some contrary evidence.

The Only Way to Do It Is to Do It

I suspect that one reason teachers don't try visualization and other unconventional approaches is that they are afraid they might not work. At a workshop on wholistic education taught by Dr. Jack Canfield a number of years ago, we learned some unusual imagery strategies. As I acknowledged at the beginning of this book, Jack made a statement which I took to heart and applied: namely, if you're afraid you won't know how to do these strategies correctly and therefore are reluctant to try, remember *The Only Way To Do It Is To Do It.*

Most teachers are probably aware of the extreme reluctance of some LD students to try something they're not sure of, for fear they might do it wrong. It's useless to try to convince them that it's OK to take chances and risk mistakes. In fact, however, if they refuse to do so, they will not make significant progress.

So it is with us adults. We must be willing to take chances if we are to become more effective teachers. If any of the ideas in this book appeal to you, I hope you will try them and not be afraid to use your own imagination and ingenuity. As your confidence grows, your enjoyment of teaching and learning will grow.

Remember:

THE ONLY WAY TO DO IT IS TO DO IT!

Appendix

Some Procedures for Using Imagery to Aid Learning

1. **Installing Spelling Words in the Mind** (Adapted from a strategy taught by Dr. Cecilia Pollack, Orton Society, N.Y.C.)

I spell the word aloud, letter-by-letter, as students visualize themselves writing it on the chalkboard or in the wet sand by the ocean. They are told to write the letters in the air at the same time, so that I can be sure they are writing them correctly.

This procedure is repeated two more times, with instructions to write each letter upon the original one and to notice how the letters become vividly clear after the third writing. Usually the students are then able to see the word clearly and spell it back for my verification. [See Chapter Three]

An occasional student might need the exercise repeated a fourth time. Surprisingly, the spelling remains accessible later, so long as students look into their minds (i.e. visualize) and spell what they actually see.

2. **Recognizing Every Word When Reading**

Sometimes, while reading aloud, a student fails to recognize a common word. At such times I will tell the student to close her eyes and visualize the problematic word. If she can't see it in her mind, I spell it aloud, and then, when the student sees the word internally, she readily reads it. I have had several students who could not generalize this skill. That is, although they could recognize each problem word after visualizing it, they couldn't read the rest of the passage in a normal way, because they would continue to have to stop and spell too many words. In this type of situation, I had to find other ways to alleviate the difficulty. [See the *Target Practice Imagery,* Chapter One]

3. Remembering the Short Vowel-Sounds

I display an outline drawing of an apple with a cursive *a* superimposed upon it. This is to encourage an association between the short sound of *a* and the first sound in *apple*. Then I recite the following words to accompany the picture: $\bar{a}$ -*apple-a*. Reciting the words rhythmically enhances the memory. Many students have trouble keeping the rythm, but I don't make a fuss over it.

Next, the students close their eyes and visualize the picture of the apple with the superimposed *a*. They indicate that they see it by putting their hand in the air. Then, while still looking at the image, they recite the rhythmic words aloud. The same strategy applies with the other vowels ($\bar{e}$ – *egg*– *e;* $\bar{i}$ –*Indian*– *i;* $\bar{o}$ –*octopus*– *o;* $\bar{u}$ –*up* – *u*),

To reinforce the learning, I start each reading lesson with a recitation of this ritual chant, with eyes open or closed. This is done individually and/or in unison until it is no longer necessary.

4. Improving Intelligence through *Image Streaming*

Tell the students to imagine a scene from Nature or to visualize their home or some other place, and simultaneously to describe it aloud in the present tense. They may see themselves in the scene and describe the action as well. If this exercise is done daily for ten minutes (with a partner or a tape recorder) one may expect an increase in intelligence to occur after two weeks (or sooner.) If the exercise is done with a group of students, they divide into pairs and describe to each other what they are visualizing.

According to Dr. Win Wenger, college students scored an even greater gain in IQ after one month of the exercises. (Win Wenger, *How to Increase Your Intelligence*. Bobbs-Merrill, 1975; Dell Books, 1976.)

In order to picture how intelligence could improve through this practice, consider the metaphor that various areas of the brain are specialized for different activities. In this case, for example, one area deals with language, while another deals with imagery. By engaging both these areas simultaneously, we strengthen or develop connections (synapses) between them. Since the connections may be considered to be correlated with intelligence, it follows that by visualizing *and* verbalizing a scene, more and stronger synapses can develop, thereby resulting in increased intelligence.

5. Improving Language Skills (See Chapter Four)

6. Comprehending the Terms *Past, Present, and Future*

See "Past Tense Dilemma." in Chapter Four.

7. Breaking through the Inability to Visualize

See the stories of *Corman* (Chapter Six) and *Berna* (Chapter Three) .

8. Developing Mature Behaviors

See Table of Contents for *Mitchel, Corinna, Cutting Class, A Hyperactive Student, Monte Misbehaves in Math Class, Defusing a Fight,* and *Tom's Prank*

9. Kinesthetic Strategy for Remembering Letter-Sounds: One Example — *SH*

First, make sure students can print *sh* correctly before beginning the imagery. Then instruct them as follows:

a. Close your eyes. See yourself printing "s...h".

b. Print "s...h" *a second time, superimposed upon the first letters. See the letters get clear.* [Ask students if they are clear. If they are not clear, have them mentally write the letters a third or even a fourth time.]

c. Look at the image of "s...h" *and say the sounds* **sh, sh.**

d. Eyes still closed, see the letters "sh" *sitting on the front half of your tongue. They make a little depression in your tongue like a hollow cup. Feel the hollow, as you say the sound,* **sh.**

e. Every day, repeat this exercise, being sure to say the sound **sh** *aloud each time. Do this every night before bedtime and many times during the day.*

10. Kinesthetic Memory for Spelling

I was tutoring a seven-year-old who couldn't remember

how to spell her last name, *Abramovitz*. It was a long name, and she would forget to include the three letters (*o,v, i*). Since the visual imaging approach was not working for her, I modeled the following behavior for her to imitate:

a. I recited the first five letters of the last name (which she already knew.)

b. Then I formed my lips into the shape of a circle while I said "O" and pointed to my lips.

c. Next I rested my upper teeth on my lower lip, as though to bite it, and said "V" .

d. For the letter I, I merely pointed to my eye and said "I." She imitated what I did and never again had a problem spelling her last name.

11. Develop Fluency in Oral Reading
Slow background music is optional.

a. I read the story aloud, sentence by sentence, as students follow silently from their own books. After each sentence, I ask if all the words are understood.

b. Then I reread the sentence, telling the students to picture the scene: The entire page is read aloud in this way.

c. Now that the words and the content are understood, I begin the story again, reading each sentence smoothly and slowly, pausing at appropriate places. Students echo my words and timing, in unison or individually, breaking the sentences into phrases when necessary.

d. Then they combine the phrases into one smooth sentence. If they still have difficulty, I read the sentence rhythmically, matching the phrasing to the music.

e. Next, the students take turns reading the story, sentence by sentence, without my modeling. They are encouraged to observe the periods for clarification of meaning.

f. If students have repeated trouble identifying a particular word, I interrupt the reading to install the word into their mind. This is done through mentally writing it, naming the imaged letters in order, pronouncing the problematic part, and then re-spelling and pronouncing the whole word while looking at it in the image.

This whole process takes time, but students seem to appreciate it.

12. Procedure for Visiting Your Wise Being— An Imagery Strategy for Solving Problems and Easing Worries

Students identify their individual problem and frame it in the form of a question to ask their Wise Being. (Example: "How can I deal with this situation?") They may choose to reveal their problem to me and the rest of the class, or keep it to themselves. I speak in a gentle voice, slowly, to allow images to unfold.

a. *"Close your eyes and see yourself outside in a beautiful place. . . Notice the scenery. . . See the colors. . . Inhale the fresh air. . . Feel the soft warm breeze on your skin. . . Hear the sounds around you."*

[This is to engage their senses and to further their relaxation and involvement in the imagery. If you are addressing more than one student, ask them to put a finger in the air to show when they have complied with each instruction.]

b. *"Notice a fluffy cloud approaching from a distance. It comes closer, closer. Now it's on the ground in front of you. See yourself step into the cloud, feeling safe and cosy.*

c. *"The cloud floats upward, carrying you, and you feel safe and happy. You notice in the distance a mountain with a castle on it. You drift towards the mountain and settle gently upon the ground in front of the castle. It's your very own private castle.*

d. *"You step out of the cloud and go up to the door of the castle. Notice what it's made of. . . how it feels. . . smells, etc.*

e. *"While the cloud waits outside, you open the door and go in. You look around and see your Wise Being waiting for you. The Wise Being is very happy to see you and hugs you with much love."*

[In order to avoid clashing with the image they get, I don't use gender pronouns. Similarly, I avoid specifying the word "person" in case their Being is an animal or angel or whatever.]

f. *"The Wise Being asks how it can help you, and you now ask the question about your problem.*

g. *"The Wise Being nods its head and reaches behind a screen (or under a table), bringing out something for you.*

[I avoid saying "a gift," because this will likely suggest a package wrapped up with a bow.]

h. *"You take what your wise being gives you* [check that this happens by asking them to nod their head] *and thank your Wise Being. Now you hug, and the Wise Being says,*

'Come back whenever you wish; I'll always be here, waiting for you.'

i. *"Now you say goodbye and leave the castle. The cloud is waiting, and softly surrounds you. It floats you back to the beautiful place."*

I do not prolong the return trip.

When the students are on the ground, they examine their gifts and (hopefully) recognize the symbolic solution to the problem. Usually they will tell the class what the gift is and almost always express pleasure and satisfaction with the message that they interpreted from the symbol. Occasionally a student does not understand the symbolism of the gift, in which case I offer whatever appropriate explanation occurs to me.

I explain to the students that this process enables them to tap into their own wisdom. Instead of being directed what to think by the teacher, they are encouraged to access the often ignored, intelligent parts of their own mind.

13. Seeing Multiplication Facts and Spellings in Imagery

This strategy is great for helping a student recall multiplication facts or spelling words quickly. The procedure follows:

See yourself walking down a hallway. . .You come to a door. Which side of the hall is it on? . . .Open the door and see a person standing behind a counter. . . Say to him, "Please get me the card with (the particular fact or word on it.)" The person gets the card and holds it up for you to see.

In almost all cases, the card shows the correct information.

In cases where it doesn't, I say to the student: *"Tell him it's the wrong information, and you want him to put it back and bring the correct one."* In cases where I've tried this, the second card has proven to be correct.

14. Using Music to Aid Long-Term Memory
Lozanov's Concert Review

This is a strategy that I learned in a course on *Suggestopedia,* as taught by Dr. Don Schuster at Iowa State University.

The Procedure: After you have taught students some new information (such as the pronunciation or definition of words), you read the list of words and their definitions again, intoning your voice against a background of slow Baroque music.

The theory behind this strategy is that music enters the long-term memory part of the mind. In so doing, the academic information is carried along with it. Hence the material is remembered at a later date. It works surprisingly well.

15. Using Pictures to Remember Spelling Words
(See examples on the following pages.)

l. Students study the picture-plus-words.

2. Next they close their eyes and see it in their minds.

3. They copy it from the mental image onto a paper.

Henceforth, when they encounter the word in print, or when they need to write it, they look into their minds and see the mental image. The theory behind this strategy is the same as in the previous one. The pictures carry the words with them into the long-term memory.

A Strategy for Remembering *of* vs *off*

1. Students study the pictures-plus-words.
2. They practice copying them from memory onto a paper, until they remember it easily.
3. When they encounter either word in print, they look into their memory bank and see the illustration with its accompanying words.

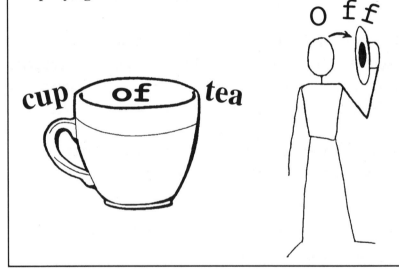

Images for the Sounds of "SH" and "S"

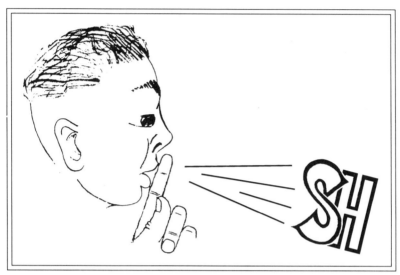

These pictures were drawn by Steve Troche, one of my students.

An Example of Using Imagery to Install the Spelling of *Girl* in Memory

Dyslexics commonly reverse the middle two letters of the word *girl*. Here is a simple line drawing that students can remember and reproduce easily. Once the picture is in their visual memory, they have no difficulty spelling *girl* correctly.

Steps for installing the spelling of "girl" in memory

1. Students look at the picture, close their eyes, and see it in their minds.
2. If they say they can't see it, tell them it's OK: they don't have to.
3. They reproduce the drawing without looking at the original. Tell those who see it in their minds to copy it from the mental image. The others copy it "from memory".
3. They check their drawing with the original for accuracy of the spelling.

Bibliography

Ahsen, Akhter. *Basic Concepts in Eidetic Psychotherapy.* New York: Brandon House, Inc., 1973.
"Eidetics: An Overview," in *Journal of Mental Imagery* vol 1. New York: Brandon House, Spring 1977.
Psycheye. New York: Brandon House, 1977.
ABC of Imagery. New York: Prohelios, 1989.

Balch, James F. and Balch, Phyllis A. "Two Brains in One?" in *Prescription for Nutritional Healing.* Garden City Park: Avery Publishing Group, Inc., 1990.

Beaumont, J.G. "Split Brain Studies and the Duality of Consciousness," in G. Underwood and R. Stevens (Eds.) *Aspects of Consciousness,* vol 2. New York: Academic Press, 1981.

Berne, Eric. *Games People Play.* New York: Grove Press, 1966.

Bonny, Helen. "Guided Imagery and Music," in *GIM Therapy—Past Present and Future Implications.* GIM Monograph #3. Baltimore: ICM Books, 1980.

Bruner, Jerome. "Introduction," p. vii, In Lev Vygotsky, *Thought and Language.* Cambridge: MIT Press, 1962.

Davis, Ronald D. with Braun, Eldon M. *The Gift of Dyslexia.* New York: The Berkley Publishing Group, 1997.

Dilts, Robert. *Roots of Neuro-Linguistic Programming*. Cupertino: Meta Publications, 1976.

Eccles, J.C. *The Understanding of the Brain*, 2nd ed. New York: McGraw-Hill, 1977.

Edwards, Betty. *Drawing on the Right Side of the Brain*. Los Angeles: J. P. Tarcher, 1979.
    Drawing on the Artist Within. New York: Simon and Schuster, 1986.

Feldenkrais, Moshe. *Body and Mature Behavior*. New York: International Universities Press, 1975.
    The Illusive Obvious. Cupertino: Meta Publications, 1981.

Fincher, Jack. *Lefties: The Origins and Consequences of Being Left-Handed*. New York: Perigee, 1980.

Gazzaniga, Michael, et al. *The Integrated Mind*. New York: Plenum, 1978.

Gleason, William. "The Founding Father of Aikido." *EastWest Journal*, October, 1983.

Houston, Jean. *Life Force: The Psycho-Historical Recovery of the Self*. New York: Delacorte, 1980.
    The Possible Human. Los Angeles: J.P. Tarcher, Inc., 1982.

Jensen, Eric. *Brain-Based Learning & Teaching*. Del Mar: Turning Point Publishing, 1995.

Kaufman, Barry Neil. *Son Rise.* New York: Ballantine, 1977.

Kershner, John. "Experiments on Dyslexics' Right-Brain Bias." *Canadian Journal of Psychology*, 33: 39-50.

Kimura, Doreen. "The Asymmetry of the Human Brain," *Scientific American*, 1973, 228 (3), 70-78.

Lambert, Bramwell, Lawther. *The Brain. A User's Manual.* New York: Putnam and Sons, 1982.

Lozanov, Georgi. *Suggestology and Outlines of Suggestopedy.* New York: Gordon and Breach, 1978.

Luria, A.R. *Higher Cortical Functions in Man.* New York: Basic Books, Inc., 1966.

Luria, A.R. and Simernitskaya. E.G. "Interhemispheric Relations and the Function of the Minor Hemisphere," in *Neuropsychologia*, 1977,15, 175-178.

Markova, Dawna. *The Art of the Possible: A Compassionate Approach to Understanding the Way People Think, Learn, and Communicate.* Conari Press, 1991.

Orton, Samuel T. *Reading, Writing and Speech Problems in Children.* New York: W.W. Norton, 1937.

Ostrander, Sheila; and Schroeder, Lynn. *Super-Learning.* New York: Delacorte Press and the Confucian Press, Inc., 1979.

Paivio, Allan, and Desrochers, Alain. "Image Memory Pegs Aid Language Recall," in *Canadian Journal of Psychology 33: 17-28.*

Pollack, Cecilia and Branden, Ann. "Odyssey of a "Mirrored' Personality," *Annals of Dyslexia*, Vol. 32, 1982.

Rawson, Margaret B. *"A* Diversity Model for Dyslexia," In G. T. Pavlidis, and T.R. Miles, *Dyslexia. Research and its Applications to Education.* London and New York: John Wiley and Sons, LTD., 1981.

Reinert, Charles P. "A Preliminary Comparison between Two Methods for   Intellectual Development., " an address to *Society for Accelerative Learning and Teaching.* San Diego, 1989.
      Increasing Intelligence by Imaging. Garvin: Glenview Press, 1989.

Seamon, J. and Gazzaniga, M. "Coding Strategies and Cerebral Laterality Effects," in *Cognitive Psychology,* 1973, 5, 249-256.

Shaffer, John T. *Psychefeedback: A Teaching Outline- The Use of Induced Guided Fantasy as a Creative Therapeutic Process.* Jacksonville, Ill.: The Well-Being Center, Inc., 1978.

Sheikh, Anees A. and Shaffer, John T. *The Potential of Fantasy and Imagination..* New York: Brandon House, 1979.

Sidtis, John; and Co-workers. "Split-brain Research," in *Science* 212: 344-346, and *The Journal of Neuroscience* 1: 323-331.

Smith, Joan M. *You Don't Have To Be Dyslexic*, Sacramento: Learning Time Products, Inc., 1996.

Sperry, R.W. "Hemisphere Deconnection and Unity in Conscious Awareness," *American Psychologist*, 1968, 23, 723-733.

Wenger, Win. *How to Increase Your Intelligence.* New York: Dell Publishing Co., Inc., 1976.
   Making Your Language a Very Very Fine Bed of Sand. Gaithersburg: Psychegenics Press, 1985.

Wenger, Win and Poe, Richard. *The Einstein Factor.* Prima Publishing, 1996.

Williams, Donna. *Like Color to the Blind.* New York: Random House, 1996.

Winner, Ellen. *Gifted Children.* New York: Basic Books, 1996.